Contents

Pearson Education Limited
Edinburgh Gate, Harlow,
Essex CM20 2JE, England
and Associated Companies throughout the world.

ISBN: 978-1-4058-4353-9

This edition first published by Penguin Books Ltd 2007

1 3 5 7 9 10 8 6 4 2

Text copyright © Penguin Books Ltd 2007
Illustrations by Mark Oldroyd

Set in 11/14pt Bembo
Printed in China
SWTC/01

Published by Pearson Education Limited in association with
Penguin Books Ltd, and both companies being subsidiaries of Pearson PLC

For a complete list of the titles available in the Penguin Readers series please write to your local
Pearson Longman office or to: Penguin Readers Marketing Department, Pearson Education,
Edinburgh Gate, Harlow, Essex CM20 2JE

Introduction

'I will prove my kindness. Go with me to the legal clerk's office, and sign this agreement for me: if you fail to repay me on time, a pound of flesh will be cut from the part of your body of my choice.'

Shylock, a greedy, unpopular money-lender, is talking to Antonio, a successful merchant who needs a loan and will agree to a very unusual condition. If Antonio cannot repay the loan in three months' time, Shylock will cut a pound of flesh from his body.

The loan is for Antonio's friend Bassanio, who also lives in the Italian city of Venice at some time during the 14th century. Bassanio wants to marry Portia, a rich, clever woman who lives outside Venice in place called Belmont. But he has a problem: he has no money and a lot of debts, and Portia has many other admirers from all over the world who are much richer than he is.

Not for the first time, Bassanio asks Antonio to lend him money. Antonio is glad to help his dear friend, but he has no cash either. All *his* money has been spent on business adventures abroad, which he hopes will make him richer. Unwilling to destroy his friend's chance of happiness, he borrows money from his enemy, Shylock. Antonio is not worried by the strange agreement. He is sure that his ships will return with a fortune from abroad before he has to repay the loan. But Bassanio is not so sure. What will happen if something goes wrong and Antonio's ships do not return? Will Shylock *really* take his pound of flesh? And why has Shylock made Antonio sign such a terrible agreement?

As the title suggests, money plays an important part in *The Merchant of Venice.* In the 14th century, Venice was the business capital of Europe. Antonio, the merchant of the title, has made a lot of money with his international business adventures. Shylock earns his living as a money-lender. Portia has been left a great fortune by her father. Bassanio's debts are the cause of Antonio's problems. And the different business methods of Antonio and Shylock are one of the reasons why the two men are enemies; unlike Shylock, whose religion allows it, Antonio never charges interest on the money that he lends.

But *The Merchant of Venice* is much more than a play about money and business. It is about human desire and its power to change people's lives. For example, money appears at first to be at the centre of Shylock's life; when his daughter runs away with her Christian lover and her father's jewellery and money, Shylock is more worried about the jewellery and money than about her safety. But later we see that his feelings of hate for Antonio are even more powerful than his love of money. He would rather have a pound of Antonio's flesh than a payment of three times the amount of the loan. His desire for revenge becomes so strong that it eventually destroys him.

Shylock is not the only person whose life changes greatly as the story progresses. At the beginning of the play, both Bassanio and Antonio seem to be worried only about money. Antonio cannot stop thinking about his ships at sea, and Bassanio wants to escape from a life of debt. But it soon becomes clear that Antonio's desire to help his friend is more important to him than making a profit, and that Bassanio will put his love for his friend even above his desire for the woman he loves.

Loyalty and love are important in the play. Bassanio and Antonio help each other whenever they can. Portia is loyal to her father's wishes and will only marry the man who passes the test that he has left behind for her admirers after his death. She also helps Antonio, who she has never met, simply because he is her future husband's friend. And both Bassanio and Gratiano get into serious trouble with their future wives when they fail an important test of loyalty.

There are many other subjects in *The Merchant of Venice* that are equally interesting and important for us in modern times. One is the difference between appearance and reality. *The Merchant of Venice* is a story full of masks, curtains, secrets and confusion! Shylock hates Antonio, but seems willing to help him and calls his cruel agreement with Antonio a 'kind offer'. Portia's admirers fail her father's test when they prefer shiny gold and silver boxes to an ordinary lead one. While Shylock's daughter dresses as a boy to escape from her father, her lover and his friends wear masks when they take her away. Portia and Nerissa also dress as men when they appear at the Duke's court. Things are never what they seem in this play!

However, the play appears to present a view from Shakespeare's time of the difference between Christians and people of other religions which is unacceptable to many people today. Antonio, a Christian, is kind and generous to his friends. Shylock, a Jew, is dishonest, greedy and cruel. Antonio and Portia teach the Christian message of forgiveness, but Shylock is only interested in punishment and revenge. Such a simple picture of good and bad may understandably be offensive today, but it reminds us that people in the past had different ideas. In the 16th century, when *The Merchant of Venice* was written, Jews were seen as outsiders because of their religion, appearance and fondness for money. People in Shakespeare's London laughed at foreigners, and it was common for them to be cruel and rude about Jews, although Jews lived more comfortably in London than in some other European cities. However, Shylock in *The Merchant of Venice* is one man, with his own character, who does not seem to have many friends, even of his own religion, and Shakespeare's plays are still performed four hundred years after his death for good reason; in so many other ways his work is timeless, which is why it is still enjoyed so much today.

The Merchant of Venice was Shakespeare's twelfth play, and it was written between 1596 and 1598. Since then, it has been performed around the world on stage, television, radio and in film. There have been many films of the play, including one by Orson Welles; mysteriously, when the film was almost completed, parts of it were lost, and have never been found again. The most recent film of

The Merchant of Venice came out in 2004, with Al Pacino as Shylock, Jeremy Irons as Antonio and Joseph Fiennes as Bassanio.

William Shakespeare (1564-1616) is the most famous writer of plays in the English language. He was born in Stratford-upon-Avon, in England. Although he went to a good school, he did not go to university. In 1582, when he was eighteen years old, he married Anne Hathaway, who was eight years older than him. They had three children. Soon after the birth of twins, Hamnet and Judith (in February 1585), however, Shakespeare left Stratford for London. Not much is known about his early life in London, but by 1592 he was famous as an actor and writer. Over the next twenty years he wrote thirty-seven plays, including *Romeo and Juliet* and *A Midsummer Night's Dream* (1594-1596), *Hamlet* (1600-1602), *Othello, King Lear* and *Macbeth* (1604-1606) and *The Tempest* (1610-1612). He also wrote many famous poems. His plays were very popular, and many of them were acted in front of King James I.

Reading and acting the play

You can read *The Merchant of Venice* silently, like every other story in a book. You will have to imagine the places, people's clothes and their voices from the words on the page.

But Shakespeare did not write *The Merchant of Venice* as literature for reading; he wrote it for actors on a stage. You can read the play in a group with other people, which is very different from silent reading. When you speak the words, you can bring the characters in the play to life. They can sound happy or sad, worried or angry. You can add silences and important noises, like the sound of music. You can also stop and discuss the play. What does this person mean? Why does he or she say that?

But you can have even more fun if you act the play. Although *The Merchant of Venice* does not have as much action as other Shakespeare plays, it has a lot of emotional speeches and arguments. It has many exciting scenes as well as several funny ones. The girls can have great fun dressing up as boys and confusing the male characters in the play!

You should think about the equipment and furniture that you will need in the different scenes. Many of the conversations happen in the streets of Venice, but in Portia's rooms, for example, you will need nice tables and chairs. You will need some special equipment, too, like knives, scales and documents. And don't forget the large curtain and three boxes in Portia's house. In some scenes there are only two or three people talking, but other scenes will be more crowded. Think, for example, where people should sit or stand in the courtroom scene in Act 4.

The Merchant of Venice is a wonderful play. You can read it or act it but, most important of all, you can have fun and enjoy it!

The Characters in the Play

THE DUKE OF VENICE
ANTONIO, a merchant of Venice
BASSANIO, Antonio's friend
GRATIANO, a friend of Antonio and Bassanio
SALERIO, a friend of Antonio and Bassanio
SOLANIO, a friend of Antonio and Bassanio
LORENZO, in love with Jessica

SHYLOCK, a Jewish money-lender
JESSICA, Shylock's daughter
TUBAL, Shylock's friend
LAUNCELOT GOBBO, Shylock's servant
OLD GOBBO, Launcelot's blind father

PORTIA, the Lady of Belmont
NERISSA, Portia's servant
THE PRINCE OF MOROCCO, Portia's admirer
THE PRINCE OF ARRAGON, Portia's admirer
BALTHASAR, Portia's servant
STEPHANO, Portia's servant

A MESSENGER from Bassanio
A MESSENGER from Antonio
TWO SERVANTS of Bassanio
A PRISON GUARD
OTHER SERVANTS in Portia's house
MUSICIANS at Portia's house
FOUR FOLLOWERS of the Prince of Morocco
SERVANTS of the Prince of Arragon
SERVANTS, LORDS and COURT OFFICIALS at the Duke's court

Bassanio

Antonio

Portia

Shylock

Gratiano

Jessica

Launcelot Gobbo

Act 1 The Agreement

Scene 1   A street in Venice

[*Antonio, Salerio and Solanio enter.*]

ANTONIO [*unhappily*]: I don't know why I'm so sad. My sadness makes me tired – and you say that it makes *you* tired, too. I don't understand what's causing it. It makes me feel so stupid that I don't recognize myself.

SALERIO: Your mind is on the ocean. There, your ships sail like kings past other merchant boats, flying across the water with their wind-filled sails.

SOLANIO: Believe me, sir, if *I* had ships on such an adventure, all *my* thoughts would be with them, too. I'd be picking grass to test the wind and studying maps for ports and roads. And every doubt and fear would make *me* sad, just like you.

SALERIO: Every time I blew on my soup, I'd worry about the harm that a wind could do at sea. I couldn't look at dust on a table without thinking of my ship hitting sand in shallow water. Every time I saw a stone church, I'd think of dangerous rocks damaging my gentle ship and filling the sea with everything that she carries. One minute you're rich, the next you have nothing. I'm not surprised that you're nervous when you think about it.

ANTONIO: Believe me, that's not true. My fortune isn't all on one ship travelling to one place. One unlucky year in business can't destroy me, so I'm not worried about that.

SOLANIO [*smiling playfully*]: So you must be in love.

ANTONIO [*shocked*]: Of course not!

SOLANIO [*confused*]: Not in love either? [*shaking his head wisely*] Nature has made some strange people. Some are born to laugh

1

at everything, but others can never smile at all. [*Bassanio, Lorenzo and Gratiano enter.*] Here comes Bassanio, your great friend, with Gratiano and Lorenzo. Goodbye. We'll leave you now in better company.

SALERIO: I'd stay with you to amuse you, but better friends than I am now make that unnecessary.

ANTONIO [*offended, to Salerio and Solanio*]: You're my very dear friends. I hope you're only leaving because you have other, more important business.

SALERIO [*to Bassanio, Lorenzo and Gratiano*]: Good morning, my lords.

BASSANIO [*surprised that Salerio and Solanio are leaving*]: Sirs, when can we enjoy your company? Why are you being so unfriendly?

SALERIO: We'll meet some other time.

[*Salerio and Solanio leave.*]

LORENZO [*to Bassanio*]: Bassanio, as you've found Antonio, we'll leave you. But don't forget where we're meeting for dinner.

BASSANIO: I'll be there.

GRATIANO [*to Antonio*]: You don't look well, Antonio. You think about the world too seriously.

ANTONIO: The world is just the world, Gratiano – a stage where every man must play his part. And mine's a sad one.

GRATIANO: Let me play the fool. Let old age come with fun and happiness. Let my heart grow hot with wine, not cold with sadness. Why should a warm-blooded man sit like a grandfather made of stone? Why should he sleep when he's awake? Why should he sink into bad-tempered old age? I love you, Antonio, and it's my love that speaks. There are some men whose faces are like silent pools. They say nothing, believing that other men will think them wise. But I'm sure that, if they spoke, they'd show themselves as fools. [*pausing, realising that he has been talking too much*] I'll tell you more of this another time. But if you want me to stop giving you my foolish opinions, you have to stop looking so sad. [*to Lorenzo*] Come, good Lorenzo. [*to Antonio*] Goodbye for now. I'll finish your lessons in happiness after dinner.

LORENZO [*to Antonio*]: Well, we'll leave you until dinner-time. I must be one of these silent, wise men, because Gratiano never lets me speak.

ANTONIO [*smiling, to Gratiano*]: You'll soon make a talker of me.

GRATIANO: That's welcome news. Silence is only good in the dried tongue of a cow, or in a young woman with no hope of marriage.

[*Gratiano and Lorenzo leave.*]

ANTONIO [*to Bassanio*]: What was all *that* about?

BASSANIO: Gratiano speaks a lot about nothing, more than any man in Venice. His reasons are like two small seeds hidden in a pile of rubbish. You can look for them all day, but when you find them, you realize that the search was a waste of time.

ANTONIO: Well, tell me now. Who's the lady that you're planning to visit in secret? You promised to tell me about her today.

BASSANIO: You must know, Antonio, that my lifestyle costs more than I can afford. In my young life I've been careless, and I'm a prisoner of my debts. To you, Antonio, I owe the most in money and in love, so I have a duty to share with you my plans to clear my debts.

ANTONIO: Good Bassanio, tell me. If the plans are as good as the man who makes them, I'll help you as much as I can.

BASSANIO [*nervously*]: In my schooldays, if I threw a ball and lost it, I'd throw another in the same direction. When I did that, I often found both balls next to each other. I'm telling you this story because my situation now is very similar. I owe you a lot but, like a selfish child, I've lost everything that I owe. Please, throw another ball in the same direction as the first. If you do, I have no doubt that I'll be able to repay all my debts.

ANTONIO: You know me well, but spend too much time on these unimportant details. I'd prefer you to waste all my money than offend me with your doubts. Tell me what you want, and it will be done. I'm ready, so speak.

BASSANIO: In Belmont there's a lady who's been left a great fortune. She's beautiful and, more important, a woman of wonderful character. Sometimes I receive lovely, wordless messages from her eyes. Her name's Portia, and she's famous all around the world. From many countries, lords and princes come to ask her to marry them. Oh, Antonio, if I had the money that they have, I'd be successful without a doubt.

ANTONIO [*shaking his head and smiling sadly*]: You know that all my fortune is at sea. I have no money at this moment, and nothing to sell. [*more positively*] But see what my good name can bring you in Venice. Borrow as much as you can – it will pay for your journey to Belmont, to lovely Portia.

[*They leave.*]

Scene 2   Belmont – a large bedroom in Portia's house.
There are large, open windows with a view of a big, sunlit garden.

[*Portia enters with her servant, Nerissa.*]

PORTIA [*looking at herself in a large mirror and shaking her head with a tired look on her face*]: Nerissa, my little body is so tired of this great world.

NERISSA: That would be true, sweet madam, if your problems were as great as your good fortune. It seems to me that people with too much are as sick as people who have too little. I'm happy, therefore, to be seated in the middle. Too much money turns the hair white too soon. People with a little less live longer.

PORTIA [*turning away from the mirror and smiling bravely*]: Those are good sentences, and well said.

NERISSA [*seriously, like a mother to a silly child*]: My advice would be better if it were taken.

PORTIA: If actions were as easy as words, poor men's homes would be princes' palaces. It's easier to teach than to follow your own advice. The brain may give us wise advice, but its voice is not as loud as our emotions. [*Shaking her head sadly, she turns away and looks out of the window.*] But thoughts like these won't help me choose a husband – if 'choose' is the right word! I can't choose who I like or refuse who I dislike. That's what happens when a living daughter must obey the wishes of her dead father. [*turning suddenly to Nerissa*] Don't you agree, Nerissa, that it's a difficult situation for me?

NERISSA [*patiently*]: Your father was a good man, and good men at their death have good intentions. He planned this test, these three boxes of gold, silver and lead, for a reason. Your future husband must be able to guess your father's intentions. He may need luck to choose correctly, but if he understands your father's meaning, he'll truly deserve your love. [*more cheerfully*] But what warmth is there in your heart for the princely men who have already come?

PORTIA: Tell me their names, and I'll give you their description.

NERISSA: First there's the prince from Naples.

PORTIA [*smiling unkindly*]: He only talks about his horses. He's very proud of his ability to shoe them himself. I wouldn't be surprised if his mother's lover earned his living making horseshoes!

NERISSA: Then there's Lord Palatine.

PORTIA: He never smiles. If he's so sad and serious now, what will he be like when he's old? [*angrily*] I'd rather marry a dead man than either of these. God defend me from these two!

NERISSA: What do you think of the French lord, Monsieur Le Bon?

PORTIA [*thinking hard for a moment*]: He has a better horse than the prince from Naples, and a more serious face than Lord Palatine. He changes his behaviour according to the situation. He's a shadow of a man with no character of his own. If I married him, I'd marry twenty different husbands. If he hated me, I'd forgive him. But if he loved me madly, I could never satisfy him.

NERISSA: And what about Falconbridge, the young lord from England?

PORTIA: I can't understand him, and he can't understand me. I have little English and he can't speak Latin, French or Italian. He's a handsome gentleman, but what can you say to a man who can't speak? And what strange clothes he wears! I think he bought his shirt in Italy, his shoes in France, his hat in Germany and his behaviour from everywhere!

NERISSA: What's your opinion of the Scottish lord, his friend?

PORTIA: He's a very generous man. The Englishman hit him and he promised to repay him when he had the chance.

NERISSA: How do you like the young German, the Duke of Saxony's nephew?

PORTIA: I hate him in the morning, but I hate him even more in the afternoon when he's drunk. At his best, he's not much worse than human; at his worst, he's not much better than an animal. If he was the last man alive in the world, I'd still run away from him.

NERISSA: What would you do if he decided to choose a box, and he chose the right one? If you refused to accept him, you would disobey your father's wishes.

PORTIA: If you put a large glass of German wine on the wrong box, I'm sure he'd choose *that*. [*urgently*] I'd do anything, Nerissa, not to marry a man with more wine in his body than blood.

NERISSA [*smiling*]: You needn't worry about any of these lords, my lady. They've told me their plans. Unless you decide to choose your husband in another way, they've all decided to return home.

PORTIA: Even if I live to be a hundred years old, I'll die unmarried unless somebody chooses the right box. But I'm glad this group of admirers are so thoughtful. I'm grateful for their absence, but I wish them a safe journey.

NERISSA: Do you remember, my lady, in your father's time, a young man from Venice – a student and a soldier?

PORTIA [*smiling excitedly*]: Yes, yes. His name was Bassanio, I think.

NERISSA: True, madam. He was, in my foolish opinion, the man who most deserved a beautiful lady.

PORTIA: I remember him well, and your good opinion of him. [*A servant enters.*] Yes? What news?

SERVANT: Your guests, madam, are waiting to say goodbye. There is also a messenger from the Prince of Morocco, who says that the Prince will be here tonight.

PORTIA: If I could welcome the next visitor as happily as I say goodbye to the last, I'd be glad of his arrival. [*unhappily to Nerissa*] Come, Nerissa. While we shut the gate on one admirer, another knocks at the door.

[*They leave.*]

Scene 3   *The Rialto, a public square in Venice*

[*Bassanio enters with Shylock the Jew.*]

SHYLOCK: Three thousand ducats*, you say?

BASSANIO: Yes, sir, for three months.

SHYLOCK [*thinking*]: For three months? Mm.

BASSANIO: As I have told you, the loan will be in Antonio's name.

SHYLOCK [*still thinking*]: In Antonio's name? Mm.

BASSANIO [*nervously*]: Will you help me or not? What do you say?

SHYLOCK [*still thinking*]: Three thousand ducats for three months, and in Antonio's name?

BASSANIO: And your answer to that?

SHYLOCK: Antonio is a good man.

BASSANIO [*surprised*]: Why should anyone believe differently?

SHYLOCK [*laughing*]: No, no, no! I mean his *money* is good. [*shaking his head seriously*] But his fortune is not safe. He has a ship sailing to Tripoli, another to India; I have also heard that he has a third sailing to Mexico and a fourth to England. But ships are only

*ducat: a gold coin used in Venice at that time

wood, sailors are only men. Just as there are land rats and water rats, there are thieves on the water as well as on the land. There is also the danger of water, winds and rocks. [*smiling at Bassanio*] But the man's name is good. Three thousand ducats? I think I can reach an agreement with him. [*thoughtfully*] And agreements must be guaranteed. I will think about how. Can I speak to Antonio?

BASSANIO: Let me invite you to dinner with us.

SHYLOCK: [*offended*]: To smell the meat of a pig? To eat impure food? I will buy with you, sell with you, talk with you, walk with you. But I will not eat with you, drink with you or speak to your God. [*looking around the square*] Who is this coming?

[*Antonio enters.*]

BASSANIO: This is Antonio.

SHYLOCK [*narrowing his eyes at Antonio and speaking bitterly to himself*]: Look at him! He reminds me of an ordinary tax-collector. I hate him because he is a Christian. But more important, I hate him because he charges no interest on his loans, so he brings down the profits of money-lending for us in Venice. But I will have my revenge on him. He hates our religion. And he complains about me in public to all the other merchants, just because I make a profit on my loans. I will never forgive him.

BASSANIO: Shylock, did you hear me?

SHYLOCK: I was thinking about the money. I do not think I have three thousand ducats at the moment. But Tubal, a Jew like me, will help me. [*suddenly smiling at Antonio*] How are you, good sir? We were just talking about you.

ANTONIO: Shylock, I never usually charge or pay interest on lent or borrowed money, but this time, to help a friend, I will break my habit. [*to Bassanio*] Have you told him yet how much you need?

SHYLOCK: Yes, yes, three thousand ducats.

ANTONIO [*to Shylock*]: And for three months.

SHYLOCK [*pretending to be surprised*]: I had forgotten – three months.

He did tell me. But now, let us think about the guarantee. I heard you say that you do not charge or pay interest on loans.

ANTONIO: That is correct.

SHYLOCK [*looking thoughtfully at Antonio*]: Three thousand ducats is a lot of money.

ANTONIO [*impatiently*]: Well, Shylock, shall we be in your debt?

SHYLOCK: Sir, I have heard you many times in this square complaining about me and my business. I have listened patiently to your insults, because all Jews have to have patience. You insult my religion, you call me a dog, and you make fun of my traditional clothes. But now it seems that you need my help. You come to me and say, 'Shylock, we need money.' You feel that you are so much better than a dog like me, and then you come to *me* for money! What should I say to you? Should I not say, 'Does a dog have money? Can a dog lend you three thousand ducats?' Or shall I bend low and whisper politely, 'Dear sir, you laughed at me last Wednesday and you called me a dog. For this friendly behaviour, of course I will lend you the money'?

ANTONIO [*angrily*]: I will not change my opinion of you. If you lend this money, lend it not to a friend but to an enemy. In this way, if I break the agreement, you can punish me more easily.

SHYLOCK: Why are you so angry? I would prefer to be friends with you and have your love. I would rather forget the insults that you have thrown at me. I would like to help you and not accept a single coin from you in interest. This is a kind offer.

BASSANIO [*confused*]: This *would* be kindness.

SHYLOCK [*with false friendliness*]: I will prove my kindness. Go with me to the legal clerk's office, and sign this agreement for me: if you fail to repay me on time, a pound of flesh will be cut from the part of your body of my choice.

ANTONIO: I will put my signature to it, and say there is much kindness in the Jew.

'If you fail to repay me on time, a pound of flesh will be cut from the part of your body of my choice.'

BASSANIO [*shocked and upset*]: You mustn't sign such an agreement for me. I'd rather have no money than that.

ANTONIO: Don't worry, it will never happen. In two months' time, before this agreement ends, I expect the return of three times the value of the loan.

SHYLOCK [*seeming to speak quietly to himself, but loud enough for the others to hear*]: What fools these Christians are. Their own business methods make them distrust the thoughts of others! [*to Bassanio*] Tell me this: how would a pound of a man's flesh profit me? It is of less value than a pound of a sheep's or cow's flesh. I make this offer as a friend. If he accepts it, good. If not, goodbye. And in return for my love, I ask you not to be unkind to me.

ANTONIO: Yes, Shylock, I will sign this agreement.

SHYLOCK: Then go to the legal clerk's office and give him the details. I will fetch the ducats immediately and will be with you soon. [*He leaves.*]

ANTONIO: The gentle Jew will soon become a Christian, he's so kind.

BASSANIO [*seriously*]: I don't trust friendly offers from villains.

ANTONIO [*cheerfully*]: Don't worry. Everything will end happily. My ships come home a month before the loan has to be repaid.

[*They leave.*]

Act 2 The Three Boxes

Scene 1 Belmont – a large room for receiving guests in Portia's house

[*Portia is with Nerissa and other servants. Music plays, and the Prince of Morocco, a dark-skinned man dressed in white, enters with four followers.*]

MOROCCO: Do not dislike me because of my skin. It is only the dark paint of the burning sun. Bring me the most beautiful young woman of the north, where the sun is too weak to destroy the ice. Let me prove to you the redness of my blood. My lady, my face has put fear into the hearts of the brave, but it has also been loved by the most beautiful young women of my country. I would not change my colour, except to steal your heart, my gentle queen.

PORTIA [*with bored politeness*]: My destiny does not allow me to follow my heart's desire. But if I were not limited by my father's wishes, you would have as much chance of winning my heart as any of the others.

MOROCCO: Even for that, I thank you. Please, therefore, lead me to the boxes to try my fortune. If this were a test of skill or bravery, I would be certain to win. But in a test of luck like this, a servant could easily beat a king. With blind fortune leading me, I might easily lose what a lesser man might win. Then I would die of sadness.

PORTIA: You must take your chance. But I warn you never to speak to me again of marriage if you choose incorrectly. If you cannot promise that, you must not choose at all.

MOROCCO: I give you my promise. Come, bring me to my destiny.

[*They leave to the sound of music.*]

Scene 2   A street in Venice

[*Launcelot Gobbo enters alone.*]

LAUNCELOT: [*shaking his head, confused by a difficult problem*]: My heart is telling me to run away from this money-lender, my master. It whispers to me all the time: 'Gobbo, Launcelot Gobbo, use your legs, be brave and run away!' But the voice of duty says, 'No, honest Launcelot, don't run away.' It advises me to stay with my master, although he's a villain. [*thoughtfully*] But if he's a villain, the voice of duty is unkind to tell me to stay with him. [*smiling as he makes a decision*] My heart's advice is much friendlier – I'll run!

[*Old Gobbo enters with a basket.*]

GOBBO: Please, sir, which is the way to Master Shylock's?

LAUNCELOT [*quietly to himself*]: It's my father! He doesn't recognize me because he's blind. [*smiling playfully*] I'll confuse him. [*to Gobbo*] Take the first right, then the first left, right again, then straight on towards his house.

GOBBO [*confused*]: Oh, that's too complicated! Can you tell me whether a man called Launcelot lives there with him?

LAUNCELOT [*quietly to himself*]: This will be fun! [*to Gobbo*] Do you mean young Master Launcelot?

GOBBO: No, sir. I'm talking about a poor man's son. His father is an honest, very poor man, although not too poor, thank God.

LAUNCELOT: Whoever his father is, we're talking about young Master Launcelot.

GOBBO: His name is Launcelot, it's true.

LAUNCELOT: You mean *Master* Launcelot?

GOBBO: Yes, Launcelot.

LAUNCELOT: So you *do* mean Master Launcelot. Well, old man, please don't talk about Master Launcelot. I've heard that he's dead. He's gone to heaven.

GOBBO [*upset*]: Oh no! The boy was everything to me.

LAUNCELOT [*moving towards the old man and speaking quietly*]: Do you know me, Father?

GOBBO [*moving backwards, afraid*]: I don't know you, young gentleman! But please tell me, is my boy alive or dead?

LAUNCELOT: Don't you recognize me, Father?

GOBBO: Sir, I'm blind! I don't know you.

LAUNCELOT: Even if you could see, you might not recognize me. It's a wise father that knows his own child. Well, old man, I'll tell you news of your son. [*going down on his knees*] Put your hand on your son's head. In the end, we'll always discover what's true.

GOBBO [*angrily*]: Please sir, stand up. I'm sure you're not Launcelot, my boy.

LAUNCELOT [*urgently*]: Stop this foolishness and put your hand on your son's head. I'm Launcelot, your son.

GOBBO: I can't believe it.

LAUNCELOT: I *am* Launcelot, the money-lender's servant. And I'm sure that Margery, your wife, is my mother.

GOBBO [*thoughtfully*]: It's true, her name is Margery. If you're truly Launcelot, then you're my own flesh and blood. [*touching Launcelot's beard*] But what a big beard you've got! You have more hair on your chin than my horse has on its tail. My God, how you've changed! How is life with your master? [*showing Launcelot the basket*] Look, I've brought him a present.

LAUNCELOT [*annoyed*]: Give him a present? It would be better to give him a rope to hang himself instead! He always keeps me hungry. [*lifting his shirt*] Look, you can count every bone in my body. [*excitedly holding his father's shoulders*] Father, I'm glad you've come. Give your present to Master Bassanio instead. At least *he* dresses his servants well. If I can't serve him, I'll run away as far as I can. [*noticing someone arriving*] Oh, I'm in luck. Here he comes now! Speak to him, Father. I can't work for Shylock another day.

[*Bassanio enters with two servants.*]

BASSANIO [*to the first servant*]: Be quick. Dinner mustn't be later than five o'clock. [*giving him some letters*] Deliver these letters, prepare the clothes and ask Gratiano to come to my house as soon as possible.

[*The first servant leaves.*]

LAUNCELOT [*pushing his father towards Bassanio*]: Speak to him, Father!

GOBBO [*nervously to Bassanio*]: God be with you, sir.

BASSANIO [*surprised*]: And with you. But what do you want?

GOBBO: Here's my son, sir, a poor boy …

LAUNCELOT [*interrupting*]: Not a poor boy, sir, but the rich money-lender's servant who would, as my father will explain …

GOBBO [*interrupting*]: He has a great desire, sir, to serve …

LAUNCELOT [*interrupting*]: Because the money-lender is unkind to me …

GOBBO [*interrupting and holding out his basket*]: I have some fresh chicken for you …

BASSANIO [*confused*]: One of you speak for both. [*to Launcelot*] What do you want?

LAUNCELOT: To serve you, sir.

BASSANIO [*surprised*]: Are you sure you want to leave a rich man's service to become the follower of a poor gentleman like me?

LAUNCELOT: He has enough money, sir, but you have goodness in you.

BASSANIO [*pleased*]: You speak well. [*to Gobbo*] Go, father, with your son. [*to Launcelot*] Leave your old master and go to my house. [*to the second servant*] Dress him well, more colourfully than the others.

LAUNCELOT [*excitedly to his father*]: So, people thought I'd never get a good job, did they? They thought I didn't have a tongue in my head? [*looking at his hand*] If any man in Italy has a luckier hand than me, I'd be surprised! Look, here's a perfect life line. [*Gobbo looks at his son's hand but cannot see anything, of course.*] And this line

15

tells me about my wives. Fifteen? Is that all? A man like me could easily manage twenty! [*to his father*] Well, if Fortune is a woman, she's been wonderful to me. Come, Father, let's go. I'll leave the greedy old money-lender immediately.

[*Launcelot leaves with Old Gobbo.*]

BASSANIO [*to his second servant*]: When everything's arranged, hurry back. I'm having dinner tonight with my best friend.
SECOND SERVANT: It will be done.

[*Gratiano enters as the second servant is leaving.*]

GRATIANO [*to the servant*]: Where's your master?
SECOND SERVANT [*pointing to Bassanio*]: Over there, sir. [*He leaves.*]
GRATIANO: Bassanio!
BASSANIO [*smiling*]: Gratiano!
GRATIANO: I have something to ask you.
BASSANIO: Whatever it is, I agree.
GRATIANO: I must go with you to Belmont.
BASSANIO: Then you must. But listen, Gratiano: you're too noisy and badly-behaved. There's nothing wrong with that in *our* eyes. But other people may think you're strange. So try to behave more politely when we go to Belmont. If you don't, I'll be misunderstood and lose all chance of success with the lady.
GRATIANO: I'll wear plain clothes, talk politely and only use a little bad language. I'll carry religious books in my pockets and look shyly at the ground. I'll even cover my face with a hat when thanks are given to God before a meal. If I don't, never trust me again.
BASSANIO [*doubtfully*]: We shall see.
GRATIANO: But not tonight. You can't judge me by what I do tonight.
BASSANIO [*laughing*]: No, you must enjoy yourself because we have friends who deserve a lot of fun. [*suddenly serious*] But go now, because I have some business.

GRATIANO: I'll see you for dinner.

[*They leave.*]

Scene 3   Venice – a living room in Shylock's house. The furniture is
expensive, but the room is dark and dusty.

[*Jessica and Launcelot enter.*]

JESSICA: I'm sorry that you're leaving my father. Our house is hell but you've made life much more interesting with your cheerful jokes. But goodbye [*giving him a coin*] – here's a ducat for you. And Launcelot, soon at dinner you'll see Lorenzo, your new master's guest. [*giving him a letter*] Give him this letter – do it secretly. So, goodbye. I wouldn't want my father to see me talking to you.

LAUNCELOT [*with tears in his eyes*]: Goodbye! Tears show what my tongue cannot say. Most beautiful lady, sweetest Jew! If a Christian did not win your heart, I would be surprised. But goodbye again. These foolish tears embarrass me. [*He leaves.*]

JESSICA: Goodbye, good Launcelot. [*turning sadly*] Oh, why am I ashamed to be my father's child? Although I share his blood, my behaviour is completely different. Oh, Lorenzo, if you keep your promise, this problem will be solved. I shall become a Christian and your loving wife. [*She leaves.*]

Scene 4   Venice – a street

[*Gratiano, Lorenzo, Salerio and Solanio enter.*]

LORENZO: No, we'll leave quietly during dinner, put on our masks and return an hour later.

GRATIANO [*worried*]: We haven't prepared this very well.

SALERIO: We haven't discussed who'll carry the torches yet.

SOLANIO: It's a terrible idea. In my opinion, it's best not to do it.

LORENZO It's only four o'clock. We still have two hours. [*Launcelot enters with a letter.*] Friend Launcelot, what's the news?

LAUNCELOT [*bending forward, holding out the letter with both hands*]: If you open this letter, sir, you may find something important.

LORENZO [*taking the letter, reading the front and smiling*]: I know the writing. It's by a lovely hand, whiter than the paper it's written on.

GRATIANO [*smiling at Solanio and Salerio*]: A message of love!

LAUNCELOT [*politely moving away*]: With your permission, sir.

LORENZO: Where are you going?

LAUNCELOT: To ask my old master, the Jew, to have dinner tonight with my new master, the Christian.

LORENZO: One minute – take this. [*giving Launcelot a coin*] Tell gentle Jessica, in private, that I'll keep my promise. [*Launcelot takes the money and leaves.*] [*to Salerio and Solanio*] Go, gentlemen, will you prepare for our masked party tonight? I already know who'll carry my torch. Meet me and Gratiano at Gratiano's house in an hour's time.

[*Salerio and Solanio leave.*]

GRATIANO: Was that a letter from Jessica?

LORENZO: I need to tell you everything. She's explained how I'll take her from her father's house tonight. She'll also bring some gold and jewels with her and she'll be dressed in boy's clothes. If her father ever goes to heaven, it will be because of his gentle daughter. [*giving Gratiano the letter and hurrying away*] Quickly, come with me. Read this as we go. Jessica will carry my torch tonight.

[*Lorenzo and Gratiano leave.*]

Scene 5   In front of Shylock's house

[*Shylock and Launcelot enter.*]

SHYLOCK [*with a voice of warning*]: Well, you'll soon see the difference between old Shylock and Bassanio … [*calling*] Jessica! [*to Launcelot*]

You won't eat as well as you did with me. [*calling again*] Jessica!

[*Jessica enters.*]

JESSICA: Did you call? What do you want?

SHYLOCK: I've been invited to supper, Jessica. [*giving her some keys*] Here are my keys. [*looking annoyed*] But why am I going? They don't like me. They're only pretending to be friendly. [*smiling bitterly*] But although I hate Christians, I can still take their food. [*to Jessica*] Jessica, my girl, take care of the house. [*pausing, changing his mind again*] I really don't feel like going. I know something bad's going to happen because I dreamt about money bags last night.

LAUNCELOT: You must go, sir. My young master is expecting you. And they have planned something for the masked party tonight.

SHYLOCK [*surprised*]: What? A masked party? [*angrily to Jessica*] Listen to me, Jessica. Lock all the doors. And when you hear their awful music in the street, stay away from the window. I don't want you to look at silly Christians with masked faces. Shut all the house's ears – I mean, my windows. The sound of this shallow foolishness will not enter my serious house. [*to Launcelot*] I'm *really* not in the mood for this tonight, but I will go. You go ahead of me. Tell them that I am coming.

LAUNCELOT: I will, sir. [*whispering to Jessica*] Madam, look out of the window for this: there will be a Christian who deserves to catch your eye. [*He leaves.*]

SHYLOCK [*annoyed*]: What did the fool just say to you?

JESSICA [*nervously*]: His words were 'Goodbye, madam', nothing else.

SHYLOCK [*relaxing*]: The silly man's kind enough, but he eats too much, is slow to learn, and is lazier than an old cat. Now he can help his new master to waste his borrowed money. Well, Jessica, go in. I'll probably be back soon. Remember, lock the doors after you and shut all the windows. [*He leaves.*]

JESSICA [*quietly angry*]: Goodbye. And if things go according to plan, soon I'll have no father, and you'll have no daughter. [*She leaves.*]

Scene 6   *Later, in front of Shylock's house*

[*Gratiano and Salerio are standing outside the house, wearing masks.*]

SALERIO: Lorenzo's late.

GRATIANO: That's strange, because lovers are usually early.

SALERIO: The birds of love fly ten times faster to a new love than to an old one.

GRATIANO: That's true. Things are usually chased with more desire than they're enjoyed.

[*Lorenzo arrives, wearing a mask.*]

LORENZO: Sweet friends, I'm sorry for the delay, but I've had important business. When *you* want to steal *your* future wives, I'll be happy to wait as long for you. [*looking at the house*] This is where my lady's father lives. [*calling*] Hello! Is anybody there?

[*Jessica, wearing boy's clothes, opens an upstairs window.*]

JESSICA: Who are you? Tell me, although I'm sure I recognize your voice.

LORENZO: Lorenzo, your love.

JESSICA: Lorenzo, you know that my love is true. But who else knows about my love for you?

LORENZO: Only heaven and you.

JESSICA [*holding out a small box*]: Here, catch this box. It's valuable. [*She throws the box down to Lorenzo.*] I'm glad that it's dark because you can't see me. I'm ashamed of my clothes. But love is blind, and lovers never recognize the silly things they do.

LORENZO: Come down, because you must be my torch carrier.

JESSICA: What? Must I hold a light to my embarrassment?

LORENZO: You look sweet even dressed as a boy. But come now, it's getting late and Bassanio's waiting for us.

JESSICA: I'll lock the doors, bring some more ducats, and be with you immediately. [*She closes the window.*]

LORENZO [*to Gratiano and Salerio*]: Oh, I love her with all my heart!

'Here, catch this box'.

She's wise, if I judge her correctly. And beautiful, if my eyes are clear. [*Jessica leaves the house.*] [*to Jessica*] Are you ready? [*to Gratiano and Salerio*] Gentlemen, let's go. Our masked friends are waiting for us.

[*Lorenzo leaves with Jessica and Salerio. Gratiano bends to tie up his shoe. Antonio arrives. He is not wearing a mask.*]

ANTONIO [*to Gratiano*]: Who's there?

GRATIANO [*standing up*]: Antonio?

ANTONIO: Gratiano! Where are all the others? It's nine o'clock and everybody's waiting for you. There'll be no masked party tonight. The wind has changed, and Bassanio will soon be on his ship. I've sent twenty people out looking for you.

GRATIANO [*taking off his mask and smiling*]: I'm glad. Nothing will give me greater pleasure than to sail away tonight.

[*Antonio and Gratiano leave.*]

Scene 7   Belmont – another room in Portia's house. There is a large curtain hiding a table in the middle of the room.

[*Portia, the Prince of Morocco and their servants enter to the sound of music.*]

PORTIA [*to one of her servants*]: Pull the curtain open and show the Prince the three boxes. [*The servant opens the curtain. There are three boxes on a table.*] [*to the Prince of Morocco*] Now make your choice.

MOROCCO [*looking at the first box*]: This first box is made of gold, and the writing says, [*reading*] 'This box will give men whatever they desire.' [*looking at the second box*] The second is made of silver, and it says, [*reading*] 'This box will give men whatever they deserve.' [*looking at the third box*] This one is only made of lead, and it has this warning: [*reading*] 'A man might lose everything if he chooses this box.' [*to Portia*] How shall I know if I have chosen correctly?

PORTIA: One of them contains my picture, Prince. If you choose that, then I am yours.

MOROCCO: Let God guide my decision. [*looking thoughtfully at the third box*] This box says that I might lose everything. But why should I lose everything just for a box of lead? [*looking at the second box*] This one says that I will get what I deserve. In my opinion, I deserve a lot, but it may not be enough to win the lady. Let's see once more this box of gold. [*reading again*] 'This box will give what many men desire.' [*smiling*] Yes, that's the lady! All the world desires her. From the four corners of the earth they come to kiss her feet. Such a beautiful jewel can never be found in anything less than gold. [*to Portia*] Give me the key. This is the box I choose.

PORTIA [*giving him the key*]: There, take it, Prince. And if my picture is in the box, then I am yours.

[*The Prince of Morocco opens the box.*]

MOROCCO [*unhappily*]: Oh! What have we here? The bones of a dead man's head, and in one of its empty eyes there is a message. [*reading the message*]

'Not all shining things are gold;
Often you have heard that told.
Many men from many lands
Want to have me in their hands.
But under every golden stone
There is just a pile of bones.
To wise men, this is no surprise.
Your love has failed, my friend. Goodbye.'

[*sadly to Portia*] There is too much sadness in my heart for a long goodbye. I will go immediately.

[*The Prince of Morocco leaves with his servants to the sound of music.*]

PORTIA [*bored*]: Another quick goodbye. [*to one of her servants*] Close the curtain. Let's hope all the others like him choose gold, too.

[*The servant closes the curtain. Portia and her servants leave.*]

Scene 8 A street in Venice

[*Salerio and Solanio enter.*]

SALERIO: I saw Bassanio sail away. Gratiano went with him, but Lorenzo stayed here. He was seen in a small boat with Jessica, and Shylock's heard the news.

SOLANIO [*laughing*]: I've never heard anyone as confused or angry as the old money-lender. He was shouting in the streets: 'My daughter! Oh, my ducats! Oh, my daughter! She's run away with a Christian! I want justice! The law! My ducats and my daughter! Two bags of ducats, stolen from me by my daughter! And two precious jewels! Where's the law! Find the girl! She has my jewels and my ducats!'

SALERIO [*laughing too*]: All the boys in Venice are following him, shouting about his jewels, his daughter and his ducats.

SOLANIO [*seriously*]: Antonio must be careful. If he doesn't return his loan on time, he'll pay for this.

SALERIO [*worried*]: That's true. A Frenchman told me yesterday about a ship from our country that had sunk in the sea between England and France. I hope that it isn't Antonio's.

SOLANIO: You should tell Antonio what you've heard. But do it gently – you don't want to upset him.

SALERIO: Antonio's the kindest man in the world. I saw him say goodbye to Bassanio. Bassanio promised to hurry home, but he answered, 'Don't ruin your business because of me. Stay there as long as you like. And don't think about my agreement with the money-lender. Be happy, and think only about love.' There were tears in his eyes when he said goodbye to Bassanio.

SOLANIO: Let's go and find him. With all his problems, he'll need some cheerful company.

[*Salerio and Solanio leave.*]

24

Scene 9   Belmont – the same room in Portia's house as in Scene 7

[*Nerissa comes in with a servant.*]

NERISSA: Quickly! Pull the curtain straight. The Prince of Arragon will be here very soon.

[*Portia arrives with the Prince of Arragon and his servants to the sound of music.*]

PORTIA [*pointing to the curtain*]: There are the three boxes, my lord. If you choose the box with my picture in it, we shall be married immediately. But if you fail, my lord, you must leave without delay, without a word.

ARRAGON: I have promised to do three things: first, I will never tell anyone which box I choose. Next, if I fail, I will never ask another woman to marry me. Lastly, if I fail, I will leave immediately without complaint.

PORTIA: Everybody makes the same promises.

ARRAGON: Let fortune guide me to my heart's desire! [*A servant opens the curtain. The Prince of Arragon walks to the table and looks at the three boxes.*] Gold, silver and ordinary lead. [*He reads the writing on the lead box.*] 'A man might lose everything if he chooses this box.' [*shaking his head*] You will have to look more attractive than that before I choose you. [*looking at the next box*] What does the golden box say? [*reading*] 'This box will give what many men desire.' [*repeating thoughtfully*] 'What many men desire …' That 'many' may mean the silly crowds who judge everything by appearance. They only learn what their foolish eyes teach them and never look beyond that. I will not choose what many men desire, because I am different from other people. I do not belong with their shallow-minded crowds. [*looking at the third box*] So, to you, the box of silver. Let me see what your message says. [*reading*] 'This box will give men whatever they deserve.' [*smiling*] That is well said. Too many people are given land, power and money without

25

earning them. How many forgotten people would be suddenly admired if success went to the ones who deserve it? How many commanders would be commanded? How many poor people would become lords? Yes, this is my choice. 'This box will give men whatever they deserve.' I will have my reward. Give me the key for this and let me unlock my fortune.

[*A servant gives the Prince of Arragon the key. He opens the silver box and stares into it in shocked silence.*]

PORTIA [*quietly to herself*]: You don't need to pause for as long as that!

ARRAGON [*with shocked disbelief*]: What's here? A picture of an ugly fool with a message for me! I will read it. Oh, how unlike Portia you are! How unlike my hopes and dreams! 'This box will give men whatever they deserve.' Did I deserve no more than a fool's head? Is this my prize? Is this the only reward that I deserve?

PORTIA: You cannot defend yourself and judge yourself at the same time.

ARRAGON: What does it say? [*reading*]

'Many fools alive are dressed

In silver, it is true.

So find another wife, my friend.

My head belongs to you.'

I shall look even more like a fool if I stay here any longer. I came here with one fool's head, and I am leaving with two. [*to Portia*] Goodbye. I shall keep my promise. I will suffer my misfortune with patience.

[*Arragon leaves with his servants.*]

PORTIA: The flame of the torch has burnt another bird's wings. Oh, these fools! When they choose, they are only wise enough to lose.

NERISSA: The old words are true. Destiny decides whether we find love or death.

PORTIA: Close the curtain, Nerissa.

[*A messenger arrives.*]

MESSENGER [*excitedly*]: Madam, a young man from Venice has arrived at your gate. He has brought expensive gifts from his master, who will arrive here soon. Oh, an April day was never so sweet …

PORTIA [*unenthusiastically*]: That's enough, please. I'm half-afraid you'll tell me next that he's a member of your family! [*to Nerissa*] Come, Nerissa. Let's see who the God of Love has sent me now.

NERISSA [*looking up, holding her hands together*]: Oh, please let it be Bassanio!

[*Portia and Nerissa leave.*]

Act 3 Bad News

Scene 1   A street in Venice

[*Solanio and Salerio enter.*]

SOLANIO: Now what news?

SALERIO: There are reports that Antonio *has* lost a ship between England and France.

SOLANIO [*worried*]: Let's hope the reports are wrong.

SALERIO: Or if not, let's hope that he loses no more.

SOLANIO: Let our wishes reach heaven before the Devil hears them. [*Shylock arrives.*] [*whispering to Salerio*] Here comes the Devil in the mask of a Jew. [*to Shylock*] How are you, Shylock? What news among the merchants?

SHYLOCK [*angrily*]: You know very well that my daughter has flown away.

SALERIO: Of course we do. I know the man who made her wings.

SOLANIO: And Shylock knew that the young bird was ready to fly. It is only natural for young birds to leave their home.

SHYLOCK: She can go to hell.

SALERIO: She will, if the Devil is her judge.

SHYLOCK: My own flesh and blood!

SALERIO: There is more difference between your flesh and hers than there is between ink and snow. But tell us, have you heard whether Antonio has lost a ship at sea?

SHYLOCK: That is another bad piece of business for me! A man with no money, a beggar who used to walk so proudly on the square! Let him remember his guarantee. He thought I was just a greedy money-lender. And he is a Christian who never charges or pays interest on loans. Let him remember his guarantee.

SALERIO [*shocked*]: You wouldn't take his flesh, would you? How would you profit from that?

28

SHYLOCK: If it feeds nothing else, it will feed my revenge. He has insulted me a million times. He has laughed at me when I lost money, made fun of my religion, ruined my business, criticised me to my friends and made friends with my enemies. And why? Because I am a Jew. Does a Jew not have eyes? Does a Jew not have feelings? Is he not hurt when he is hit? Does he not suffer from the same diseases? Is he not warmed and cooled by the same summer and winter as a Christian is? If you cut us, do we not bleed? If you poison us, do we not die? And if you harm us, shall we not take revenge? If we are like you in everything else, we must be the same as you in this. If a Jew harms a Christian, what is his punishment? Revenge. If a Christian harms a Jew, what should *his* punishment be – according to Christian example? Of course, revenge! I will practise what I have been taught, but I will do it better than my teachers.

[*A messenger from Antonio arrives.*]

MESSENGER [*to Salerio and Solanio*]: Gentlemen, my master Antonio is at his house and desires to speak to you both.
SALERIO: We have been looking for him everywhere.

[*Salerio and Solanio leave with the messenger. Tubal arrives.*]

SHYLOCK: Tubal, what news from Genoa? Have you found my daughter?
TUBAL: I have tried, but without success.
SHYLOCK [*angrily*]: One jewel cost me two thousand ducats in Frankfurt! And there are other precious stones. Why can't my daughter be dead at my feet with the jewels in her ear? No news of them? Why not? And I don't know how much I have spent on this search. The thief has escaped with so much, but it costs so much to find the thief! If there is no satisfaction, there is no revenge! All the bad luck is on *my* shoulders, all the tears are in *my* eyes!
TUBAL: But other men have bad luck, too. I heard in Genoa that Antonio …

SHYLOCK [*interrupting excitedly*]: What? Bad luck?

TUBAL: … has lost a ship sailing from Tripoli.

SHYLOCK [*happily*]: Thank God! Is it true?

TUBAL: I spoke to some of the sailors who escaped.

SHYLOCK [*laughing*]: Thank you, good Tubal. Good news, good news! Ha, ha!

TUBAL [*seriously*]: I have also heard news of your daughter. In one night in Genoa, she spent eighty ducats.

SHYLOCK [*staring at Tubal with shock and disbelief*]: That is like a knife to my heart. I shall never see my gold again. [*crying*] Eighty ducats in one night? [*shouting*] Eighty ducats!

TUBAL: I came to Venice with other men who have lent Antonio money. They all believe that he will be unable to pay his debts.

SHYLOCK [*smiling cruelly*]: I am glad. I shall punish him. I shall make him suffer.

TUBAL: One man showed me a ring that your daughter had given him for a monkey.

SHYLOCK [*angrily*]: To hell with her! *You* are making *me* suffer, Tubal. My wife, Leah, gave me that ring before I was married. It is more precious to me than a million monkeys!

TUBAL: But Antonio has certainly lost everything.

SHYLOCK [*calming down*]: Yes, that is true. That is very true. And if he cannot repay his loan on time, I will have his heart. [*excitedly*] Go, Tubal, fetch me a legal clerk. Then meet me at my house.

[*Shylock and Tubal leave quickly.*]

Scene 2 Belmont – the room in Portia's house with the three boxes

[*Bassanio, Portia, Gratiano, Nerissa and servants enter.*]

PORTIA [*to Bassanio*]: Wait a day or two before making your choice. If you choose the wrong box, you'll have to leave, and I don't want to lose your company. If you stayed here for a month or two, I could teach you how to choose correctly. [*sadly*] But I'm not allowed to, and you might choose the wrong box. [*annoyed at Bassanio, who looks confused*] Don't look at me like that! My heart is yours, but I'm not free to follow what my heart desires. So, although I'm yours, I'm *not* yours. [*urgently*] Prove destiny wrong. Let destiny go to hell, not me. [*sadly*] But I've been talking too much. I only do it to keep you here longer, to delay the sad moment of choice.

BASSANIO [*bravely*]: Let me go and meet my destiny.

PORTIA [*nervously*]: Go then. I'm locked in one of the boxes. If you love me, you'll choose the right one. [*to Nerissa and the servants*] Stand back. Let music play while he makes his choice. If he loses, the music will allow him a beautiful exit. If he wins, it will celebrate his success.

[*Music plays. Nerissa opens the curtain and Bassanio studies the three boxes.*]

BASSANIO [*thoughtfully*]: Appearances are often false, but the world still believes the tricks they play. In law, the worst lies are masked by clever argument. In religion, the worst mistakes are excused by words in a church. All bad things can look good on the outside. A coward can make himself look brave with a thick beard and a serious face. An ugly woman can buy a beautiful face from a bottle. An attractive shore can hide a dangerous sea. A pretty mask can trick even the wisest man. Therefore, gold and silver, I will not touch you. [*resting his hand on the box of lead*] But you, ordinary lead, your paleness touches my heart. I will choose you, and let happiness be my reward!

PORTIA [*quietly excited*]: How all my other feelings – doubt, fear and jealousy – fly away! Oh love, be gentle with me. Don't fill me with your happiness too quickly …

BASSANIO [*opening the box of lead*]: What do I find here? A picture of beautiful Portia! [*looking at the picture*] What living thing has come so near to perfection? Are her eyes moving, or is it my imagination? Her soft lips are brushed with sugar breath, and in her hair the painter has made a golden cloud to catch the hearts of men. But even this fine painting is just a shadow of the real thing. [*putting down the picture and picking up a written message*] Here's the message – my future and my destiny. [*reading*]

'You are brave and very wise

Not to trust your foolish eyes.

As this fortune falls to you,

Be happy – look for nothing new.

If you are well pleased with this,

Turn to where your lady is

And win her with a loving kiss.'

[*to Portia*] A gentle message. Dear lady, I am shaking with happiness. But I won't believe that this is true until you say that it is.

PORTIA: Lord Bassanio, if I were a thousand times richer and more beautiful, I'd still be glad to be yours. Although I may seem to have everything, I'm just a simple girl at heart. I've studied little and have experienced even less, but I'm not too old to learn. I was the mistress of this great house and of my servants; but now this house and these servants belong to you, as I do, my lord. [*giving Bassanio a ring*] I give them with this ring. If you ever lose it or give it away, it will mean the end of our love.

BASSANIO: Madam, I am lost for words. But if this ring ever leaves my finger, then all life will leave my body.

NERISSA: My lord and lady, it is now time for others to speak, to congratulate you both on your happiness.

GRATIANO: My lord Bassanio, and my gentle lady, I wish you all the happiness in the world. And on the day of your wedding, please allow me to be married, too.

BASSANIO [*surprised*]: Of course! But have you found a wife?

GRATIANO [*looking at Nerissa*]: Thank you, my lord – *you* have found

'Dear Lady, I am shaking with happiness.'

me one. My eyes, my lord, can see as clearly as yours. You saw the lady, and I saw her servant. You loved, I loved. Your destiny was in those boxes, and mine was, too. With words of love, I won this promise: I would win her love if you won the love of her lady.

PORTIA [*to Nerissa*]: Is this true, Nerissa?

NERISSA [*shyly*]: It is, madam.

BASSANIO [*to Gratiano*]: Gratiano, this isn't a joke, is it?

GRATIANO [*seriously*]: It is not, my lord.

BASSANIO [*smiling*]: Then we shall be glad to share our wedding day with you. [*Lorenzo enters with Jessica and Salerio.*] Lorenzo and Salerio, welcome [*suddenly uncertain*] – if welcome is in my power to give. [*to Portia*] With your permission, I'd like to welcome my friends and countrymen.

PORTIA [*smiling*]: They are very welcome.

LORENZO [*to Portia*]: Thank you. [*to Bassanio*] I hadn't intended to visit you here, but I met Salerio and he asked me urgently to come with him.

SALERIO: That's true, my lord, and there was a reason for it. Antonio wants to see you.

[*Salerio gives Bassanio a letter.*]

BASSANIO: Before I open it, tell me how my good friend is.

SALERIO: His letter will tell you.

[*Bassanio opens the letter.*]

GRATIANO [*to Nerissa*]: Greet Jessica warmly; make her welcome. [*shaking Salerio's hand*] What news from Venice? How's Antonio? I know he'll be glad about our success. We've won our prize.

SALERIO [*sadly*]: But he has lost his.

PORTIA: Something in the letter has stolen the colour from Bassanio's face. It must be about a dear, dead friend. What else could turn such a strong man pale? [*to Bassanio*] What? Something worse? Bassanio, I'm half of you. I must freely have half of whatever this paper brings you.

BASSANIO: Oh, sweet Portia, these are the most unpleasant words that were ever written on paper! Gentle lady, when I first showed my love to you, I freely told you I had nothing. But it was worse than that. I'd asked a dear friend to help me. He borrowed money from his enemy to help me. This letter is the body of my friend, and every word is bleeding with his blood. [*to Salerio*] Is it true, Salerio? Have all his business adventures failed? Didn't even one ship escape the awful touch of those merchant-murdering rocks?

SALERIO: Not one, my lord. In addition to that, even if he had the money to repay the Jew, Shylock would not accept it. I've never known a man who is greedier for revenge. Twenty merchants, the Duke himself, and all the lords of Venice have tried to argue with him. But he refuses to change his mind about his cruel demand for punishment and justice.

JESSICA: I've heard him say to Tubal, his friend, that he'd rather have a pound of Antonio's flesh than twenty times the money that he owes him.

PORTIA [*to Bassanio*]: This man seems to be in a lot of trouble. Is he a good friend of yours?

BASSANIO: My dearest friend, the kindest man on earth.

PORTIA: How much does he owe the Jew?

BASSANIO: Because of me, three thousand ducats.

PORTIA: Is that all? Pay him six thousand and destroy the agreement. I'd double it before a friend as good as this lost a hair for helping you. Come to church with me and marry me. Then go to Venice with your friend. I'll give you gold to pay this debt twenty times. But first, let me hear your friend's letter.

BASSANIO [*reading*]: 'Sweet Bassanio, I've lost all my ships and people are becoming cruel. I must honour my agreement with the Jew, which means I'll lose my life. All debts between you and I will be forgotten if I can see you at my death. But I leave the choice with you. If your love for me can't make you come, don't let this letter change your mind.'

PORTIA: Oh, love, leave your business here and go without delay.

BASSANIO: As I have your permission to leave, I'll go immediately. But I'll hurry back to you as soon as I can.

[*Bassanio, Portia, Nerissa, Gratiano, Lorenzo, Jessica and Salerio leave.*]

Scene 3 A street in Venice

[*Shylock, Solanio and Antonio enter with a prison guard.*]

SHYLOCK [*to the prison guard*]: Take care of the prisoner. Don't talk to me about forgiveness. This is the fool who lent money without profit.

ANTONIO: Please listen to me, Shylock.

SHYLOCK [*angrily*]: You'll be punished for your debt! You made an agreement with me! You called me a dog for no reason. So if I'm a dog, be careful of my teeth! The Duke will give me justice.

ANTONIO: Please listen to me.

SHYLOCK: I'll have my guarantee! I refuse to listen to you, so say no more. I'm not a fool. I won't allow myself to be beaten by Christian beggars. Don't follow me – I'll have no more conversation. You'll honour your agreement! [*He leaves.*]

SOLANIO: He's the cruellest man that has ever lived!

ANTONIO [*without energy*]: Leave him alone. I won't ask him any more. He wants my life, and I know why: when people borrowed money from him, I often helped them with their debts. He hates me because of that.

SOLANIO: I'm sure the Duke will never force you to honour the agreement.

ANTONIO: The Duke can't deny the course of law. If he does, foreign businessmen will say that our laws are dishonest. Then our city will lose business from abroad. [*in a weak voice*] So go. My problems have weakened me so much that I won't even have a pound of flesh to give. [*to the prison guard*] Ask Bassanio to come and see me pay his debt. After that, I don't care what happens.

[*Antonio, Solanio and the prison guard leave.*]

36

Scene 4   Belmont – the same room in Portia's house as in Act 2 Scene 1

[*Portia enters with Nerissa, Lorenzo, Jessica and Balthasar, one of her servants.*]

LORENZO [*to Portia*]: Madam, Antonio is a good man and your husband's dearest friend. If you knew him, you'd be very proud of the help that you offer him.

PORTIA: If Antonio is my husband's closest friend, he must be an excellent man. Therefore he deserves the best help that I can give. But this makes me sound too proud of myself – let's talk of other things. Lorenzo, I want you to manage my business in my husband's absence. I've made a secret promise to stay alone with Nerissa until our husbands' return. There's an old house two miles away, and we are going to stay there. Please do not refuse me this request.

LORENZO: Madam, with all my heart I shall obey your commands.

PORTIA: My servants already know my plans, and will accept you and Jessica instead of Lord Bassanio and myself. So, goodbye until we meet again.

LORENZO: Goodbye and good luck.

JESSICA [*to Portia*]: I wish you every happiness.

PORTIA [*to Jessica*]: Thank you, and I wish you the same. Goodbye, Jessica. [*Lorenzo and Jessica leave.*] [*to Balthasar*] Now, Balthasar, as I have always found you honest and loyal, take this letter. [*She gives him a letter.*] Hurry to Padua and give it to my cousin, Doctor Bellario. He will give you some clothes and a letter for me. Bring them as quickly as you can to the place where the boat leaves for Venice. Be quick! I shall wait for you there. [*Balthasar leaves.*] [*to Nerissa*] Come, Nerissa. We've got work to do that I haven't told you about yet. We'll see our husbands before they think about us.

NERISSA [*confused*]: Will they see us?

PORTIA [*playfully*]: They will, Nerissa, but they won't recognize us. I promise you: when we're dressed as men, I'll be a better man than you. I'll wear my knife more bravely but with style. I'll deepen

37

my voice and walk in a fearless, manly way. I'll invent stories of dangerous fights and tell lies about ladies who died of broken hearts because of me. I know a thousand silly male tricks, and I'll practise them all! But come with me. I'll tell you all my plans while we're travelling. We have a twenty-mile journey to make today.

[*Portia and Nerissa leave.*]

Scene 5   A garden in Belmont

[*Launcelot and Jessica enter.*]

LAUNCELOT: Yes, it's true. The crimes of a father are passed down to his children, so I'm worried about you. I've always been honest with you, so I'm telling you my thoughts now. I really think you're going to hell. You have only one hope, although it's only a small one.

JESSICA [*amused*]: And what hope is that?

LAUNCELOT: You can hope that the Jew isn't your real father.

JESSICA: So I must hope that the crimes of my *mother* are passed down to me!

LAUNCELOT [*shaking his head sadly*]: Unfortunately, you've been sent along the road to hell by your father *and* your mother. You lose *both* ways.

JESSICA: I'll be saved by my husband. He's made me a Christian.

LAUNCELOT: That's even worse! We already have enough Christians. This endless production of new Christians will put up the price of pigs. If everybody ate pork, soon there wouldn't be enough pork to eat.

[*Lorenzo arrives.*]

JESSICA [*to Launcelot*]: I'll tell my husband what you've said. Here he comes.

LORENZO [*smiling at Launcelot*]: I'll soon become jealous of you, Launcelot, if you keep hiding like this in corners with my wife.

JESSICA [*playfully*]: You needn't worry, Lorenzo. Launcelot and I have had an argument. He tells me that there's no forgiveness for me in heaven because I'm a Jew's daughter. He also says that you're not a good member of society. By turning Jews into Christians, you increase the price of pork.

LORENZO [*to Launcelot*]: Only fools can play with words as well as this. Soon, only monkeys will be able to talk, and silence will be more intelligent than words. Go inside, my good man, and tell them to prepare for dinner.

LAUNCELOT: That's already done, sir. Their stomachs are all ready.

LORENZO [*impatiently*]: Then tell them to get dinner ready.

LAUNCELOT: That's been done too, sir. They only need to cover the table.

LORENZO: So will you put a cover on, sir?

LAUNCELOT [*looking at his clothes*]: I'm already covered.

LORENZO [*shaking his head with disbelief*]: You argue over every word, as usual. Why do you have to complicate everything? [*urgently*] Please, try to understand simple language. [*speaking slowly and clearly*] Go to your colleagues, tell them to cover the table with a cloth and serve the meat. Then we can come in for dinner.

LAUNCELOT: The meat will be covered, sir, and the table will be served. [*He leaves.*]

LORENZO: My God, what a fool! His memory's full of good words, and I know many fools in higher places who are exactly like him. They use clever words, but they still make no sense. [*smiling*] But how are you, Jessica? Tell me, what's your opinion of Lord Bassanio's wife?

JESSICA: She's wonderful beyond words. Lord Bassanio must repay destiny with an honest life for giving him such a lovely wife. He's found the happiness of heaven here on earth. If, on earth, he doesn't deserve it, he should never be allowed into heaven.

LORENZO: You have a husband as perfect as Bassanio's wife.

JESSICA [*laughing*]: You can ask *my* opinion about that!

LORENZO: I will soon. First, let's go to dinner.

JESSICA: No, let me say nice things about you while I'm in the mood.

LORENZO [*shaking his head*]: Save it for the dinner table. Then whatever you say, I'll be able to eat it with my food.

[*Jessica and Lorenzo leave, holding hands and laughing.*]

Act 4 The Judgment

Scene 1 Venice – a court of justice

[*The Duke, some Lords, Antonio, Bassanio, Salerio and Gratiano enter with the Duke's servants and court officials.*]

DUKE: Is Antonio here?

ANTONIO: I am ready.

DUKE: I am sorry for you. You have come to answer an inhuman enemy with no pity or forgiveness in his heart.

ANTONIO: I have heard, my lord, that you have tried to soften his demands. But the law is on his side and he will not change his mind. Therefore I intend to meet his anger with patience, and will suffer his violence quietly.

DUKE [*loudly*]: Call the Jew into court.

SALERIO: He is ready at the door. He is coming, my lord.

[*Shylock enters and stands in front of the Duke.*]

DUKE: Shylock, we all believe that you are not really as cruel as you seem. We believe that you are waiting until the last minute before you show some forgiveness. Instead of asking for a pound of this poor merchant's flesh, you will free him from his agreement. Looking with pity on him, you will find a little kindness in your heart. We all expect a gentle answer.

SHYLOCK: I have already informed you of my purpose, my lord: the agreement must be honoured. You ask me why I would rather have a pound of flesh than three thousand ducats. My only answer is that it is my wish. Does that answer your question? What would you think if a rat was in my house, and I paid ten thousand ducats to have it poisoned? Are you satisfied with my answer yet? Some men hate the sight of a pig's head on a table with an apple in its

41

mouth. Some go mad at the sight of a cat. Others feel ill when they hear the sound of musical pipes. Desire is the master of our emotions. Our feelings are governed by what we like or hate. So here is your answer: there is no good reason for hating a pig's head, a harmless cat or the sound of musical pipes, but we have no choice. We are forced to offend when we are offended. Similarly, I can give no reason for my actions except that I hate Antonio. Therefore, although I am making no profit from our agreement, I want him to honour it fully. Does *that* answer satisfy you?

BASSANIO [*angrily*]: This answer doesn't excuse your cruel behaviour, you unfeeling man.

SHYLOCK [*coldly*]: I do not have to please you with my answers.

BASSANIO: Do all men kill the things they do not love?

SHYLOCK: Does any man hate the thing he would not kill?

BASSANIO: We don't hate everything that offends us.

SHYLOCK: What? Would you let a rat bite you twice?

ANTONIO [*to Bassanio*]: You're wasting your time arguing with him. Why don't you stand on a beach instead and ask the sea to go back? Or ask a wild dog why it kills young sheep? Or tell mountain trees to stop whispering in the wind? You have more chance of success with these things than with trying to soften his Jewish heart. So please stop all this arguing. Let me be judged quickly, and let Shylock have his wish.

BASSANIO [*producing a bag of money*] [*to Shylock*]: For your three thousand ducats, here are six.

SHYLOCK: If you offered me *sixty* thousand ducats, I would not accept it. The agreement must be honoured.

DUKE: How can you hope for forgiveness if you offer none?

SHYLOCK: But what do I have to fear if I have done nothing wrong? You have among you many unpaid workers. You give them the same hard treatment that you give your dogs and horses. Shall I say to you, 'Let them be free! Let them marry your children?' You will answer, 'The workers are ours.' Similarly, therefore, I will answer you. [*pointing to Antonio*] This man's pound of flesh, which I demand, is dearly bought. It is mine, and I will have it. If you deny it, nobody will trust the laws of Venice again. I expect justice. Shall I have it?

DUKE: I have sent for Bellario, a wise doctor, to listen to these arguments. If he does not come today, I have the power to close this court.

SALERIO: My lord, a messenger has arrived with letters from the doctor, who has just arrived from Padua.

DUKE: Bring us the letters. Call the messenger.

BASSANIO [*to Antonio*]: Be brave, Antonio! Shylock will have *my* flesh, blood and bones before he puts a finger on you.

ANTONIO [*smiling sadly*]: The weakest kind of fruit falls soonest to the ground. Let me do the same. You're more useful alive, Bassanio, so you can remember me after my death.

[*Nerissa enters, dressed as a man.*]

DUKE [*to Nerissa*]: Do you come from Padua, from Bellario?

NERISSA [*in a deep voice*]: From both, my lord. Bellario sends his greetings.

[*While Nerissa gives the Duke a letter, Shylock has secretly taken out his knife and is inspecting its edge.*]

BASSANIO [*noticing the knife, to Shylock*]: Why are you sharpening your knife so enthusiastically?

SHYLOCK [*pointing to Antonio*]: To cut the payment from that beggar there.

GRATIANO [*to Shylock*]: Your knife is sharp, but not as sharp as your cruel behaviour. Can no words touch your heart?

SHYLOCK: No, none that you are clever enough to say.

GRATIANO [*angrily*]: To hell with you! Your existence poisons the name of justice.

SHYLOCK [*smiling coldly*]: You cannot destroy my agreement with your angry words. You waste your breath by speaking so loud. Think before you speak, or your brain will go soft. The law is on *my* side.

DUKE: In this letter, Bellario says that he has sent a young but wise doctor to our court. [*to Nerissa*] Where is he?

NERISSA: He is waiting for your permission to enter, my lord.

DUKE: I give it with pleasure. [*to his servants*] Go and give him a warm welcome, then bring him here. [*Three servants leave.*] Now the court will hear Bellario's letter. [*reading*] 'Unfortunately, I am very ill and am unable to come. But when your messenger arrived, I had a young Roman doctor with me, whose name is Balthasar. I told him about the problem between Shylock, the money-lender, and Antonio, the merchant, and he understands the situation perfectly. With your permission, my lord, he will come to the court instead of me. Please pay no attention to his age. I have never known such a wise head on such young shoulders.' [*Portia enters dressed as Balthasar, a Doctor of Law*] You have heard the words of wise Bellario, and now here comes the young doctor. [*to Portia*] Give me your hand. Did old Bellario send you?

PORTIA [*in a deep voice*]: He did, my lord.

DUKE: You are welcome. Are you familiar with the details of this problem?

PORTIA: I have studied them carefully. [*looking around the court*] Which is the merchant here, and which is the money-lender?

DUKE: Antonio and old Shylock, step forwards.

PORTIA [*to Shylock*]: Is your name Shylock?

SHYLOCK: It is.

PORTIA: Although your demand is strange, it is supported by the law of Venice. [*to Antonio*] You are in debt to this man, are you not?

ANTONIO: I am.

PORTIA: Is it true that you signed this agreement with him?

ANTONIO: It is.

PORTIA: Then Shylock must show forgiveness.

SHYLOCK [*angrily*]: Why must I? Tell me that.

PORTIA: The quality of forgiveness is the most important quality of all. It falls like gentle rain from heaven. It is precious to the one who gives it and to the one who receives it. It makes a man a

'The quality of forgiveness is the most important quality of all.'

king more than a golden palace does. Earthly power becomes more heavenly when a king's justice is guided by forgiveness. Therefore, Shylock, although justice is on your side, think about this: although justice will be done, none of us will be rewarded. If we ask for forgiveness, we must learn to give forgiveness, too. If you make this merchant honour his agreement, according to this court of Venice he must lose his life.

SHYLOCK: To hell with forgiveness! I want justice. The agreement must be completely honoured.

PORTIA [*to the court*]: Is he not able to repay the money?

BASSANIO: Yes. I can offer the court twice the amount of his debt. If that is not enough, I can pay ten times the amount. If even this is not enough, it would seem that revenge is more important than justice. [*emotionally*] This court has the power to change the law on this occasion. If you want to do a great right, it is necessary to do a little wrong. [*pointing to Shylock*] Deny this cruel devil his revenge.

PORTIA [*calmly*]: That is impossible. No power in Venice can change a traditional law. It would be a bad example, and other, similar requests would follow. It cannot happen.

SHYLOCK [*enthusiastically*]: Oh, wise young judge, how I admire you!

PORTIA: Please let me see the agreement.

SHYLOCK [*giving Portia the agreement*]: Here it is, good doctor.

PORTIA [*taking the agreement*]: Shylock, you have been offered three times the amount of the loan.

SHYLOCK: A promise has already been made by me to heaven! Shall I break such a promise? No, not for Venice!

PORTIA [*after reading the agreement*]: It is true that the debt has not been paid, and lawfully you can ask for a pound of flesh from near the merchant's heart. Show kindness. Accept three times your money, and let me destroy this document.

SHYLOCK: You can destroy it, but only when the debt is paid according to the guarantee. You seem to be a wise judge. You know the law, and you have shown a good understanding of the situation. Make your judgment according to the law, of which you are a well-deserving supporter. No power in the tongues of men will make me change my mind. The agreement must be honoured.

ANTONIO: I ask this court with all my heart to give its judgment now.

PORTIA [*to Antonio*]: Justice must be done. Prepare your chest for his knife.

SHYLOCK [*excitedly*]: Oh, wise judge! Oh, excellent young man!

PORTIA: The purpose of the law is to obey every word of this agreement.

SHYLOCK: That is very true. Oh, honest judge! You are so much more experienced than you look!

PORTIA [*to Antonio*]: Open the front of your shirt.

SHYLOCK: Yes, show me your chest. It is in the agreement, is it not, good judge? 'Nearest his heart' – those are the exact words.

PORTIA: That is true. Do you have scales to weigh the flesh?

SHYLOCK [*producing them from under his seat*]: I have them ready.

PORTIA: Have your doctor ready, Shylock, to stop him bleeding to death.

SHYLOCK [*suddenly confused*]: Does it say that in the agreement?

PORTIA: Not exactly, but what does that matter? It would be good of you to show some kindness.

SHYLOCK [*taking the agreement from Portia, reading it and shaking his head*]: I cannot find it; it is not in the agreement.

PORTIA [*to Antonio*]: You, merchant, have you anything to say?

ANTONIO: Only a little. I am ready and well-prepared. [*to Bassanio*] Give me your hand, Bassanio, and God be with you. You must not feel guilty or unhappy about this. Destiny is behaving more kindly than usual. She usually lets men live longer than their happiness, but she has saved me from suffering a sad old age. Remember me to your wife and tell her about Antonio's end. Say how I loved you and speak well of me after my death. Be sorry, but only for losing a friend. I am not sorry for paying your debt. If the Jew cuts deeply enough, I will pay your debt immediately with all my heart.

BASSANIO: Antonio, I am going to be married to a wife who is as dear to me as life itself. But life itself, my wife and all the world are not more precious to me than your life. I would lose them all to save you.

PORTIA [*coldly*]: Your wife would give you little thanks for that if she were here to hear you make the offer.

GRATIANO: I have a wife who I love dearly. But it would be better if she were in heaven. Then she could ask the heavenly powers to change this crazy Jew's mind.

NERISSA [*coldly*]: I am glad that *your* wife cannot hear *you*. If she could, there would be trouble at home.

SHYLOCK [*annoyed*]: Christian husbands! I would prefer my daughter to marry a murdering thief than to have a Christian husband. But we are wasting time. Make your judgment now.

PORTIA [*to Shylock*]: A pound of that merchant's flesh is yours. The court has decided, and it is the law.

SHYLOCK [*smiling*]: Most honest judge!

PORTIA: You must cut this flesh from his chest. The law allows it, and it is the court's decision.

SHYLOCK [*excitedly*]: Oh, wise judge! [*waving his knife at Antonio*] Come, prepare for your punishment!

PORTIA [*holding up her hand to interrupt*]: One minute, there is something else. This agreement allows you flesh, but not a single drop of blood. The exact words are 'a pound of flesh'. So take your payment, take your pound of flesh. But when you cut it, you must not take one drop of Christian blood. If you do, your land and money will become the property of Venice, by law.

GRATIANO [*happily*]: Oh, honest judge! Listen to him, Shylock. Oh, wise judge!

SHYLOCK [*confused*]: Is that the law?

PORTIA [*showing him a legal document*]: You can read the law yourself. You wanted justice. I promise you, therefore, that you will have more justice than you expected.

SHYLOCK [*unhappily*]: All right. I accept the first offer. Pay me three times the amount of the debt and free the Christian.

BASSANIO [*holding up the bag of money*]: Here is the money.

PORTIA [*to Bassanio*]: Wait! The money-lender must have total justice. He is only allowed payment according to the agreement.

GRATIANO [*laughing with happiness*]: Oh, Shylock! What an honest, clever judge!

PORTIA [*to Shylock*]: Prepare, therefore, to cut off the flesh. Do not take any blood, or take more or less than exactly one pound. If the scales show even a hair's weight less or more, you will die and all your property will go to the state.

GRATIANO [*laughing more loudly*]: Now, unbeliever, you are beaten!

PORTIA [*to Shylock*]: Why are you pausing? Take your payment.

SHYLOCK [*quietly to Antonio*]: Repay the main debt and let me go.

BASSANIO [*holding up a smaller bag of money*]: I have it ready for you. Here it is.

PORTIA: He has refused it in the open court. He is only allowed justice according to the words of the guarantee.

GRATIANO [*breathless from laughing*]: Shylock, isn't this the wisest judge in the world?

SHYLOCK [*with disbelief*]: Can I not even have the loan returned to me?

PORTIA: You will only have what is owed you according to the guarantee. Take it, and accept the responsibility.

SHYLOCK [*angrily*]: Then let the Devil take him! I have nothing more to say. [*He starts to leave.*]

PORTIA: Wait! You have another law to obey. According to the law, if a foreigner tries to take the life of a citizen of Venice, half of the foreigner's property belongs to that citizen. The other half belongs to the state and the offender's life can only be saved by the Duke. In my opinion, you are in that situation now. You have planned to take the life of this citizen [*pointing to Antonio*]. You have broken the law. Fall on your knees, therefore, and ask the Duke for forgiveness.

GRATIANO [*to Shylock*]: Ask for permission to hang yourself. But as all your property now belongs to the state, you'll have to ask the state to buy you some rope.

DUKE [*to Shylock*]: I want you to see the difference between our attitudes. Therefore, I am offering you your life before you ask for it. Half of your property goes to Antonio, the other half comes to the state.

SHYLOCK [*tearfully*]: No, take my life! Do not leave me with that! You take my house when you take everything that supports it. You take my life when you take everything that allows me to live.

PORTIA [*to Antonio*]: What kindness can you show him, Antonio?

GRATIANO: A free piece of rope! Nothing else, in God's name!

ANTONIO [*to the Duke*]: With your permission, my lord, let him keep one half of his property. After his death, I will give the other half to the gentleman who recently stole his daughter. He must, though, do two things: he must become a Christian, and he must sign an agreement to leave everything to his daughter and Lorenzo after his death.

DUKE: He will do this, or he will be punished with death.

PORTIA [*to Shylock*]: Are you satisfied, Shylock? What do you say?

SHYLOCK [*quietly*]: I am satisfied.

PORTIA [*to a court assistant*]: Write the necessary document.

SHYLOCK [*to the Duke*]: Let me go now, please. I am not well. Send the document to me and I will sign it.

DUKE: Go, but be sure to do it.

GRATIANO [*to Shylock*]: If I were the judge, I would send you to the hangman's platform, not the church.

[*Shylock leaves.*]

DUKE [*to Portia*]: Sir, I would be pleased if you could come with me to dinner.

PORTIA: Forgive me, my lord, but I must return to Padua tonight. I have to leave immediately.

DUKE: I am sorry that you are so busy. [*to Antonio*] Be grateful to this gentleman because, in my opinion, you owe him much. [*He leaves with his servants, the other lords and court officials.*]

BASSANIO [*to Portia*]: My dear sir, your wise actions today have saved my friend and me from serious punishment. As payment, [*holding out a bag of money*] please accept this money, which we were going to give to Shylock.

ANTONIO: More than this, I will be in debt to you in love and service for ever.

PORTIA [*refusing the money*]: By saving you I am satisfied, and therefore I am already well paid. I hope that we will meet again. I wish you well, but now I must leave.

BASSANIO: Dear sir, if you will not accept any payment, you must let us give you something as a sign of our thanks. Name two things, please. Do not refuse me this.

PORTIA: As you have forced me, I agree to your request. Give me your gloves, and I will wear them in your memory. [*Bassanio takes off his gloves and gives them to Portia.*] And for your love, I will take this ring from you. Do not take back your hand; I will not take anything else. As a sign of love, you cannot refuse me this.

BASSANIO [*embarrassed*]: This ring, sir, is of little value. I would be too ashamed to give you this.

PORTIA: I will accept nothing else. Only this.

BASSANIO: There is more to this ring than its value. I will find the most expensive ring in Venice and gladly give it to you. But please do not take this.

PORTIA [*pretending to be displeased*]: I see, sir, that you should be more careful with your promises. You showed me how to be a beggar, but now you show me how a beggar should be answered.

'And for your love, I will take this ring from you.'

BASSANIO: Sir, this ring was given to me by my wife. When she put it on, she made me promise not to sell, lose or give it away.

PORTIA [*coldly*]: Many men say that to excuse themselves from making gifts. If your wife were wise, she would understand how much I have deserved this ring. She would not be your enemy for ever if you gave it to me. Well, peace be with you!

[*Portia and Nerissa leave.*]

ANTONIO: Bassanio, let him have the ring. Which is more important – his reward and my love, or your wife's command?

BASSANIO [*giving Gratiano the ring*]: Go, Gratiano, run after him and give him the ring. Then bring him, if possible, to Antonio's house. Hurry! [*Gratiano leaves quickly with the ring.*] [*to Antonio*] Come, let's go to your house immediately. Then we'll both leave for Belmont early tomorrow morning.

[*Antonio and Bassanio leave.*]

Scene 2   A street in Venice

[*Portia and Nerissa enter, still dressed as men.*]

PORTIA [*giving Nerissa a document*]: Find the Jew's house, give him this document and let him sign it. We'll leave tonight and be home a day before our husbands. Lorenzo will be pleased with this document. He and Jessica will be rich after Shylock's death.

[*Gratiano runs in.*]

GRATIANO [*breathlessly*]: Sir, I have managed to find you. My Lord Bassanio has changed his mind. He has sent this ring to you and asks you to accept his invitation to dinner.

PORTIA [*surprised*]: I do not believe it. [*taking the ring*] Please tell him that I accept his ring most gratefully. Now, would you kindly show my assistant Old Shylock's house?

GRATIANO: With pleasure.

NERISSA [*to Portia*]: Sir, could I speak to you? [*whispering*] I'll see if I can get my husband's ring. *He* promised to keep *his* for ever, too.

PORTIA [*whispering*]: You will, I promise you. Then we'll have great fun hearing how they gave the rings away! Now, go. You know where to find me.

NERISSA [*to Gratiano*]: Come, sir, will you show me to this house?

[*Nerissa and Gratiano leave. Portia follows.*]

Act 5 The Rings

Scene 1 Belmont — a tree-lined path by moonlight, outside Portia's house.

[*Lorenzo and Jessica enter, hand in hand.*]

LORENZO [*dreamily*]: The moon is shining brightly. On nights like this, when the sweet wind gently kisses the trees without a sound, great heroes of the past dreamt of their loves. And on a night like this, Jessica ran away from her father and escaped from Venice with her love as far as Belmont.

JESSICA [*playfully*]: On a night like this, Lorenzo spoke great words of love, but none of them were true.

LORENZO [*playfully*]: And on a night like this, pretty Jessica made fun of her love, but he forgave her.

JESSICA: I'd continue this conversation if we were alone, but I can hear somebody's footsteps.

[*Stephano arrives.*]

LORENZO: Who comes so fast in the silence of the night?

STEPHANO: A friend.

LORENZO: A friend? What friend? What's your name?

STEPHANO: Stephano is my name, and I am bringing news that my mistress will be here at Belmont before sunrise. She is in no hurry. Whenever she sees a church, she stops and asks God for a happy marriage.

LORENZO: Who is with her?

STEPHANO: Only her servant. But please tell me, has my master returned yet?

LORENZO: He has not, and we have heard no news of him. [*to Jessica*] But let's go inside, Jessica, and prepare a big welcome for the mistress of the house.

[*Launcelot runs in.*]

LAUNCELOT [*loudly*]: News! News! Hello? News!

LORENZO: Who is calling?

LAUNCELOT [*unable to see Lorenzo in the darkness*]: Have you seen Master Lorenzo? News! News!

LORENZO [*impatiently*]: Stop shouting, man! Come here.

LAUNCELOT [*confused*]: Where? Where?

LORENZO [*loudly*]: Here!

LAUNCELOT [*not recognising Lorenzo*]: Tell him there's good news from my master. He will be here before morning.

[*Launcelot leaves.*]

LORENZO [*to Jessica*]: Sweet lady, let's go in and wait for their arrival. [*pausing*] But why should we go in? [*to Stephano*] My friend Stephano, tell them inside the house about your mistress's arrival, then bring out your musicians. [*Stephano leaves.*] How sweetly the moonlight is sleeping on the grass. Let's sit here and listen to the music. Soft peacefulness and the night sing beautifully together. Sit, Jessica. [*pointing to the sky*] Look how the floor of heaven is shining with stars. Even the smallest of them makes the loveliest music in our hearts. But while our hearts are imprisoned in the muddy clothing of our flesh, we cannot hear it. [*The musicians arrive and the moon disappears behind a cloud.*] [*to the musicians*] Come, wake the moon with your gentle instruments. And with your sweetest touches, reach your mistress's ear and guide her home with music.

[*The musicians start playing.*]

JESSICA: Sweet music always makes me quiet.

LORENZO: That's because it touches your soul. Young horses jump and play together madly and noisily, which is natural behaviour for all young things. But if, by chance, they hear the sound of a bell or any music touches their ears, they stop. You can see them standing perfectly still, their wild eyes softened by the sweet power of music. A man with no music in his heart is a man who can be disloyal, dishonest and greedy. His heart is as shadowy as night and his feelings are as dark as the road to hell. Never trust a man like that. Listen to the music.

[*Portia and Nerissa arrive and stop a short distance from Lorenzo and Jessica.*]

PORTIA [*pointing ahead*]: Look – that's the torch burning in my hall. You can see the light of its flame from so far away. In the same way, a good act shines in a bad world.

NERISSA: When the moon was shining, we couldn't see the torchlight.

PORTIA: Smaller lights always disappear when a greater light shines. An ordinary man in royal clothes shines as brightly as a king until a real king arrives. Then the ordinary man's importance empties itself, like a small river, into the ocean. [*surprised*] But listen! Music!

NERISSA: They are the musicians of your house, madam.

PORTIA: Music sounds much sweeter at night than by day.

NERISSA: Silence gives it that magic, madam.

PORTIA: If a songbird of the night sang with all the other birds by day, it would not sound so special. Habit deafens us to so many beautiful things. [*The moon appears from behind the cloud.*] [*to the musicians*] Enough!

[*The music stops*]

LORENZO: That's Portia's voice, if I'm not mistaken. [*standing up*] Dear lady, welcome home.

PORTIA: We've been asking God for our future husbands' safe, quick return. Are they back yet?

LORENZO: Not yet, madam. But a messenger came earlier to say that they were coming.

PORTIA [*to Nerissa*]: Go inside, Nerissa. Tell my servants not to say anything about our absence. [*to Lorenzo and Jessica*] And you mustn't say anything either.

[*There is the sound of voices in the distance.*]

LORENZO: The men are here; I can hear their voices. Don't worry, madam. We won't say anything.

[*Bassanio, Antonio and Gratiano arrive.*]

PORTIA [*to Bassanio*]: Welcome home, my lord.

BASSANIO: Thank you, madam. Please welcome my friend. [*introducing Antonio*] This is Antonio, my dearest friend.

PORTIA: Sir, you're very welcome to our house. But words cannot show you how welcome you are, so I will make no long speeches.

GRATIANO [*who has been arguing quietly with Nerissa, now speaks loudly*]: I promise by the moon above that you're wrong about me! Honestly, I gave it to the judge's clerk.

PORTIA [*laughing*]: Ha-ha. An argument already! What's the matter?

GRATIANO: It's about a circle of gold, a silly ring that she gave me. There were some words on it, like the words of a simple poem: 'Love me, and never leave me.'

NERISSA [*angrily, but enjoying herself*]: What do *you* know about poems? You promised that you'd wear it until the hour you died. Even after death, you said, it would never leave your finger. How could you be so careless? A judge's clerk! I expect he isn't even old enough to have a beard!

GRATIANO: He will have one, if he grows to be a man.

NERISSA [*laughing with disbelief*]: Oh, yes, if a *woman* lives to be a man!

GRATIANO [*holding up a hand*]: With this hand, I gave it to a young man, a kind of boy, a short boy no taller than yourself – the judge's clerk. He was a silly boy, and he asked me for it as payment. I couldn't refuse him.

PORTIA [*to Gratiano*]: You were wrong to be so careless with your

58

'I promise by the moon above that you're wrong about me.'

wife's first gift. Promises put it on your finger and trust made it part of your flesh. I gave *my* love a ring and made him promise to keep it for ever. [*looking at Bassanio*] And here he stands. I trust him completely – all the money in the world couldn't make him take it from his finger. Honestly, Gratiano, you've been too unkind to your wife and caused her too much pain. In her place, I'd be mad with anger.

BASSANIO [*quietly to himself*]: It would be better to cut my left hand off. Then I could say that I lost the ring defending it.

GRATIANO: My lord Bassanio gave *his* ring to the judge. The judge asked for it, and he deserved it, too. And then the boy, his clerk, who worked very hard, asked for mine. They wouldn't accept anything else – only the two rings.

PORTIA [*to Bassanio*]: What ring did *you* give, my lord? I hope it wasn't the one you received from me.

BASSANIO: If I could lie to hide my mistake, I would. [*holding out his hand*] But you can see that my finger has no ring on it. It's gone.

PORTIA [*appearing angry, but enjoying herself*]: Is there nothing true at all in your dishonest heart? I'll never come to your bed until I see the ring!

NERISSA [*to Gratiano*]: And I'll never come to *yours* until I see *mine* again!

BASSANIO: Sweet Portia, you don't understand who I gave the ring to or why. You don't realize how unwillingly I gave it when I had no choice. If you did, you wouldn't be so angry with me.

PORTIA: And *you* don't understand the true meaning of the ring. You don't realize half the qualities of the woman who gave it to you. If you did, you'd understand how wrong it was to give it away. You say that you gave the ring unwillingly? What kind of man would accept as a gift something so precious to its owner? No, Nerissa has taught me what to believe. Without a doubt, you gave it to a woman!

BASSANIO [*shocked*]: I promise you, madam! No woman has it. I gave it to a doctor of law, who refused three thousand ducats and asked for the ring. I refused him at first and sent him away unhappy, although he'd saved my dear friend's life. What should I say, dear lady? I had to send it after him. Embarrassment and politeness gave me no choice. I couldn't allow myself to be so ungrateful. Forgive me, good lady! But I believe that, in my position, you'd do exactly the same.

PORTIA: I warn you never to let that doctor come near my house. I loved that ring and you promised to keep it, but now *he* has it. Therefore, I'll become as free with my gifts as you have been, and I won't refuse him anything. No, not my body or my husband's bed. I shall meet him, I'm sure of it. So I advise you never to leave me alone at night. Watch me carefully. If you don't, I warn you that *I* have a precious gift to give. I'll let that doctor share my bed.

NERISSA [*to Gratiano*]: And his clerk can share mine. So I advise you strongly never to leave me alone.

GRATIANO: If I see him near you, I'll break the young man's pen!

ANTONIO [*upset by the arguing*]: I am the unhappy reason for these arguments.

PORTIA [*warmly*]: Sir, do not be upset. You are still very welcome.

BASSANIO: Portia, forgive me for my actions, although I could do nothing else. In front of these good friends, I promise you, even as I see myself twice in your two lovely eyes …

PORTIA [*to the others, interrupting Bassanio*]: Did you hear that? In my eyes he sees himself twice. One Bassanio in each eye. [*to Bassanio*] If *both* of you promise me, I *might* believe you.

BASSANIO [*urgently*]: Please, listen to me. Forgive me for this mistake, and I promise that I'll never break another promise.

ANTONIO [*to Portia*]: Recently I guaranteed my life to help your husband. I would be dead now without the help of the man who has your husband's ring. Now I am ready to make another guarantee. I promise on my *soul* that your husband will never be disloyal to you again.

PORTIA: I accept your guarantee. [*giving Antonio a ring*] Give him this. Tell him to be more careful with it than he was with the last one.

ANTONIO [*taking the ring and giving it to Bassanio*]: Here, Bassanio. Promise to keep this ring.

BASSANIO [*shocked*]: But it's the same one that I gave to the doctor!

PORTIA: I got it from him. Forgive me, Bassanio. He gave it to me because I allowed him to share my bed.

NERISSA [*to Gratiano*]: And forgive me, my gentle Gratiano. [*giving Gratiano his ring*] The judge's clerk gave me *this* because I allowed him to share *mine*.

GRATIANO [*upset*]: This is like rebuilding roads in summer when there's nothing wrong with them. Have our wives taken lovers before their husbands even deserved it?

PORTIA: There's no need to use language like that. You're both in shock. [*giving Bassanio a letter*] Here's a letter from Doctor Bellario in Padua. Read it when you have time. It says that Portia was the doctor of law, and Nerissa was her clerk. Lorenzo here is our witness. He knows we left for Venice at the same time as you and have only just returned. I haven't even gone inside the house yet. [*to Antonio*] Antonio, I have better news for you than you expect. [*giving Antonio a letter*] Read this letter and you'll learn that three of your ships succeeded in their business and have safely returned. I won't tell you how I managed to get this letter.

ANTONIO [*surprised*]: I'm speechless!

BASSANIO [*to Portia, with disbelief*]: Were you the doctor and I didn't recognize you?

GRATIANO [*to Nerissa, shocked*]: Were you the clerk who intends to be my wife's lover?

NERISSA [*laughing*]: Yes, but it will never happen – because he isn't really a man!

BASSANIO [*smiling at Portia*]: Sweet Doctor, you can share your bed with me. When I'm away, you can sleep with my wife.

ANTONIO [*to Portia*]: Sweet lady, you have given me my life in more ways than one. [*holding up the letter*] It says here that my ships have safely returned.

PORTIA [to Lorenzo]: And Lorenzo, my clerk has some good news for you, too.

NERISSA: Yes, and I won't charge him for it. [giving Lorenzo a document] Here is a gift for you and Jessica from her father. After his death, you will receive all his money and property.

LORENZO [surprised]: Dear ladies, this is food from heaven for hungry people.

PORTIA: It's almost morning. I'm sure you want to hear more about these events. Let's continue this conversation inside. We promise to answer all your questions honestly.

GRATIANO: I agree. And my first question for Nerissa is this: does she want to wait until tomorrow night, or does she want to go to bed now, only two hours before sunrise?

But for me, while I live, the most important thing
Is to keep safely forever Nerissa's ring.

[Everybody goes into the house.]

ACTIVITIES

Act 1

Before you read

1 *The Merchant of Venice* is one of Shakespeare's most famous plays.
   a What do you know about the story of the play?
   b What other Shakespeare plays do you know? What are they about? Are they amusing or sad?
2 Look at the Word List at the back of the book. Which words are:
   a for people?
   b about money and business?
3 Read the Introduction to the play and answer these questions.
   a Who is Antonio afraid of and why?
   b Which of these words <u>do not</u> describe Shylock?
      greedy   Christian   kind   unforgiving   villainous   poor
   c Choose the correct answer.
      • The people in the play live in *England / France / Italy*.
      • The play is about *love and death / loyalty / madness*.
      • The play was written after *Romeo and Juliet / Hamlet / Macbeth*.
   d Act 1 is called 'The Agreement'. What is the agreement and who makes it? Is it a sensible agreement? Why (not)?

While you read

4 Answer each question with one of these names:
   Salerio   Solanio   Gratiano   Bassanio   Nerissa   Portia
   Shylock   Antonio.
   a Who thinks that too much money is a bad thing.
   b Who is often careless with money.
   c Who refuses to eat with Antonio.
   d Who criticizes Antonio's attitude to life.
   e Who has many admirers.
   f Who reminds Antonio of the dangers at sea.
   g Who jokes about Antonio's mood.
   h Who lends money for no profit.

After you read

5 Finish the sentences below, using these words:

borrow debts fortune guarantee interest loan money
owe profits

a Bassanio plans to clear his ..... .

b Bassanio says, 'I've lost everything that I ..... .'

c Portia has been left a great ..... .

d Bassanio does not have as much ..... as Portia's other admirers.

e Antonio tells Bassanio to ..... as much as he can.

f Antonio never charges ..... , which damages other money-
lenders' ..... .

g Shylock wants a ..... for the money he lends Antonio.

h Antonio receives a ..... of 3,000 ducats from Shylock.

6 Are these sentences true or false? Correct the ones that are wrong.

a Bassanio has never borrowed money from Antonio before.

b Portia is angry with her father.

c Portia describes five admirers.

d Portia can speak French, Italian and English.

e Portia hopes that the Prince of Morocco is lucky.

f Shylock does not like Antonio but admires his business methods.

g Antonio refuses to pay Shylock interest on the loan.

h Antonio feels nervous about the guarantee that he gives Shylock.

7 Work with another student. Discuss these questions.

a Why does Bassanio tell Antonio the story about the lost ball?

b Why is Shylock unwilling to accept Bassanio's invitation to dinner?

c Why doesn't Shylock like Antonio?

d What do you think of Antonio's attitude to Shylock? Is Shylock
right to feel angry?

e What guarantee does Shylock want for his loan? Why does he say
it is a 'kind offer'?

8 Take the part of one of these characters. Tell the class how you feel
and why at the end of Act 1.

Antonio Bassanio Portia Nerissa Shylock

9 Work with another student. Take the parts of Portia and her father, before his death. Have this imaginary conversation.

Student A: You are Portia's father. Describe the test you have planned for her future husband. Explain why it is a good idea.

Student B: You are Portia. You do not agree with his test because you want to choose your own husband. Tell your father why.

Act 2

Before you read

10 Discuss these questions with another student. What problems might there be between these people?

a Portia and the Prince of Morocco

b Shylock and his servant

c Shylock and his daughter

d Antonio and Shylock

While you read

11 Who is speaking? Who are they speaking to?

a 'My destiny does not allow me to follow my heart's desire.'

.... / ....

b 'I've heard that he's dead.'

.... / ....

c 'You've made life much more interesting.'

.... / ....

d 'This problem will be solved.'

.... / ....

e 'It's a terrible idea.'

.... / ....

f 'The sound of this shallow foolishness will not enter my house.'

.... / ....

g 'There'll be no masked party tonight.'

.... / ....

h 'You don't want to upset him.'

.... / ....

i 'Did I deserve no more than a fool's head?'

.... / ....

After you read

12 Match each name on the left with a description on the right. Give reasons for your answers.

    a The Prince of Morocco   **1)** easily confused

    b Launcelot   **2)** noisy and impolite

    c Old Gobbo   **3)** happy and in love

    d Gratiano   **4)** ashamed and dishonest

    e Jessica   **5)** playful and foolish

    f Shylock   **6)** bad-tempered and worried

    g Lorenzo   **7)** proud and brave

13 Finish these sentences, using the words below.

amusing   excited   foolish   happy   kind   sad   sweet   worried

    a Lorenzo thinks that Jessica looks ..... .

    b Gratiano is ..... about missing the masked party.

    c Solanio and Salerio think that Shylock's situation is ..... .

    d Salerio is ..... about news from France.

    e Salerio thinks that Antonio is a ..... man.

    f Antonio was ..... when he said goodbye to Bassanio.

    g The Prince of Arragon thinks that many people are ..... .

    h Nerissa is ..... about the messenger's news.

14 Discuss these questions with another student. What do you think?

    a Do you feel sorry for Shylock? Why (not)?

    b Is Jessica right to leave her father without telling him? Why (not)?

    c Who would be a better husband, the Prince of Morocco or the Prince of Arragon? Why?

Act 3

Before you read

15 Discuss this question with another student. Will these people be happy in the next act? Why (not)?

Antonio   Bassanio   Shylock   Lorenzo and Jessica   Portia

While you read

16 Put these in the order they happen. Number them 1–7.

    a Portia gives Bassanio a ring.   .....

    b Shylock plans his revenge.   .....

    c Portia meets Jessica.   .....

    d Bassanio hears bad news.   .....

    e Portia and Nerissa leave Belmont. .....

    f Bassanio leaves Belmont.   .....

    g Antonio is taken to prison.   .....

After you read

17 One word in each sentence is wrong. Which word is it?
What is the correct word?

    a Shylock has been taught about revenge by Jews.

    b Shylock wants to punish Lorenzo.

    c Shylock is told that Jessica exchanged his ring for a cat.

    d Portia wants Bassanio to choose the box immediately.

    e Bassanio chooses the lead box because it looks pretty.

    f Antonio's problems have strengthened him.

    g Portia wants Gratiano to manage her business.

    h Portia sends her servant to Venice to see her cousin.

18 Rearrange these words to finish these sentences. Who is speaking?
What are they talking about?

    a 'It's only natural
      home / young / to / their / birds / for / leave.'

    b 'If you
      us / bleed / we / not / cut / do?'

    c 'That's
      like / my / a / knife / heart / to.'

    d 'All bad
      good / outside / the / on / can / things / look.'

    e 'This
      my / friend / is / body / the / letter / of.'

    f 'The Duke
      course / the / of / law / deny / can't.'

g 'I'll tell

because / who / ladies / about / lies / me / hearts / died / broken / of / of.'

h 'I know

him / who / many / like / in / are / fools / places / exactly / higher.'

19 Discuss these questions with another student. What do you think?

    a Which is Shylock more upset about: the disappearance of his daughter or of his jewels and money?

    b Who does Bassanio love more: Portia or Antonio?

Act 4

Before you read

20 Discuss these questions with another student. What do you think?

    a Will the Duke agree with Shylock or with Antonio? For what reasons?

    b What is Portia's plan?

While you read

21 Circle the correct words.

    a The law is on *Antonio's / Shylock's* side.

    b Shylock expects *justice / reward*.

    c Antonio expects *death / success*.

    d Portia is dressed as a *Doctor of Law / legal clerk*.

    e Portia thinks that the agreement must be *destroyed /honoured*.

    f Shylock can take Antonio's flesh but not his *blood / skin*.

    g The Duke says that Shylock must lose his *life / property*.

    h Portia and Nerissa plan to return home *after / before* their husbands.

After you read

22 Who talks about these things, and why?

    a rats, pig's heads and cats

    b beaches, wild dogs and mountain trees

    c unpaid workers

    d fruit falling to the ground

    e justice and forgiveness

f foreigners' property

g a free piece of rope

h gloves and a ring

23 Work with another student. Take the parts of Gratiano and Tubal, Shylock's friend. Have this imaginary conversation.

Student A: You are Tubal. You think Shylock has been punished too heavily. You also think that Antonio did not deserve to escape punishment. Explain why.

Student B: You are Gratiano. You think that Shylock deserved worse punishment. Explain why.

24 Work in pairs. Choose one of the pictures in Acts 1–4.

a Who are the characters?

b Where are they?

c Who else is there?

d What happened to the characters before this scene?

e What is happening now?

f Take the parts of two of the characters in the picture. Think about how you are feelilng and what you want to say. Then set out the scene in your own words.

Act 5

Before you read

25 Discuss these questions with another student. What do you think?

a What problems will there be when Bassanio and Portia meet?

b How will Jessica feel when she hears what happened to her father?

c Who will be happy at the end of this story? Why?

While you read

26 Are these sentences true (T) or false (F)?

    a Portia hurries back to Belmont.   .....

    b Antonio and Portia have met before.   .....

    c There was a message on Gratiano's ring. .....

    d Bassanio denies giving his ring away.   .....

    e Antonio defends Bassanio and Gratiano. .....

    f Not all of Antonio's ships sank.   .....

    g Lorenzo and Jessica will eventually
       receive all Shylock's property.   .....

After you read

27 What problems did these people have? How were they solved?

    a Jessica, with Shylock

    b Antonio

    c Bassanio, with Portia

    d Gratiano, with Nerissa

28 Work in pairs. Have this conversation.

    Student A: You are going to make a new film of *The Merchant of Venice*. Answer your actor's questions.

    Student B: You are going to play one of the main charactes in *The Merchant of Venice*. (Choose one.) Ask the film-maker about your character. How does he/she want you to sound, behave and dress? Has he/she got any other advice for you about playing the part? Discuss – very politely – anything you don't agree with.

Writing

29 What do you learn from this play about the laws of Venice as Shakespeare imagined it? Write an information sheet for a visitor.

30 Imagine you are Shylock. Write a letter to the Duke of Venice before the courtroom scene. Explain why Antonio deserves his punishment.

31 Imagine you are Launcelot. Write a letter to Shylock, your employer. Explain why you want to work for Bassanio instead.

32 Imagine you are a reporter. Write a report of the judgment (Act 4 Scene 1) for your newspaper.

33 Imagine you are Tubal, Shylock's friend. Write a letter of complaint to the Duke of Venice about the judgment (Act 4 Scene 1). Explain why you think your friend has been unfairly punished.

34 In Act 3 Scene 2, Bassanio says, 'Appearances are often false.' How are 'false appearances' important in this story?

35 Imagine you are Shylock. After Tubal has talked to you (Act 3 Scene 1), write an angry letter to Jessica. Tell her why you are a good father and she is a bad daughter.

36 A student magazine has asked readers to write a modern short story about 'The Importance of Forgiveness'. The best one will be printed in the magazine. Write your story.

37 Bassanio and Gratiano got into trouble because they broke their promises to Portia and Nerissa about the rings. Have you ever broken an important promise? Write about it.

38 Imagine you are Shylock five years later. What has happened to you since the end of the story? How have the events of the story changed your life? Have you become a better person? Are you happy? Have you become friends again with your daughter and her husband? Write your story.

WORD LIST

beggar (n) a person who asks strangers for money in the street
clerk (n) someone who works at a desk in an office
debt (n) borrowed money that you must pay back
destiny (n) the power that controls your future
devil (n) God's most powerful enemy, according to some religions
duke (n) a man with a high position, just below a prince
flesh (n) the soft part of the body between the skin and the bones
fortune (n) good luck; a very large amount of money
guarantee (n/v) a written promise that something will be done
honour (an agreement) (v) to do what you have agreed to do
interest (n) money that is charged or paid for money that was lent
justice (n) fair treatment of people, in legal or social terms
lead (n) a heavy soft grey metal
loan (n) money that is lent
mask (n) something that covers your face in order to hide it
master (n) the male employer of a servant
merchant (n) a person who buys and sells things in large quantities
mistress (n) the female employer of a servant
monkey (n) an animal that uses its hands and tail to climb trees
owe (v) to have to repay money that you have borrowed
pork (n) the meat of a pig
precious (adj) very important to you because it is special or rare
profit (n/v) the money you get when you sell something for more than it
  cost you
revenge (n) your punishment for someone who has harmed you
rope (n) very strong, thick string
scales (n) equipment for weighing things
soul (n) the part of you that continues to exist after your death
torch (n) a long stick that is burnt at one end for light
trust (n/v) belief that someone will not lie to you or harm you
villain (n) a bad person

Penguin Readers recommends

Macbeth *William Shakespeare*

Macbeth, a brave soldier, is trusted by the Scottish king. Then a strange meeting with three witches makes him greedy for power. Macbeth wants to be king. He and his evil wife make murderous plans. But how many people will have to die before their dreams come true?

Romeo and Juliet *William Shakespeare*

Romeo and Juliet is one of the most famous love stories in the world. But it is more than a great love story. It is also about life and death, happiness and sadness, and the terrible hate between two great families. Shakespeare's beautiful tale is still as popular today as it was more than 400 years ago.

Hamlet *William Shakespeare*

Hamlet is the Prince of Denmark. His heart is filled with sadness and pain. Why? Only his two best friends, Horatio and Marcellus, know the true reason. The new king, Claudius, murdered Hamlet's father and married the young prince's mother. Will Hamlet be strong and brave enough to take revenge? Is he mad? Or does he have a secret plan?

A Midsummer Night's Dream *William Shakespeare*

This wonderful story of fairies, dreams and lovers is as popular today as it was in Shakespeare's time. In a wood outside Athens, four young people are following their dreams, while fairies play strange games with them. Their world seems unreal – but is it really very different from our own?

For a complete list of all Penguin Readers titles, please visit
www.penguinreaders.com
or contact your local Pearson Longman office.